Garden Ponds and Water Features

 AREND JAN VAN DER HORST
INTRODUCTION BY RICHARD ROSENFELD

REBO
PRODUCTIONS

© 1994 Zuid Boekprodukties, Lisse
© 1996 Published by Rebo Productions Ltd
Text: Arend Jan van der Horst
Translation: Phil Goddard for First Edition Translations Ltd, Great Britain
Jacket design and layout: Ton Wienbelt, The Netherlands
Photography: Marcel Malherbe, Frank Beekers
Photo editing: fa. Onderwater, The Netherlands
Typesetting: Computech for First Edition Translations Ltd, Great Britain

ISBN 1 901094 38 3

Contents

	Foreword	5
CHAPTER 1	Introduction	6
CHAPTER 2	The rectangular pond	16
CHAPTER 3	Round ponds	34
CHAPTER 4	Square ponds	56
CHAPTER 5	Plants for damp locations	70
CHAPTER 6	The ecology of the pond	76
CHAPTER 7	Building ponds and swimming-pools	88
CHAPTER 8	The choice of flower and leaf colour	108
CHAPTER 9	The biggest leaves of them all: the gunnera	118
CHAPTER 10	Hostas, petasites, lythrum, and other large-leafed plants	126
CHAPTER 11	Bridges	134
	Acknowledgements	144

Foreword

Water has been the key element in garden design, going right back to the very beginning. Spanish Islamic gardens were laid out as a Chahar bagh, which means a fourfold garden, with four squares sectioned off by water. Lotus flowers grew in the middle. At the Generalife Palace garden, in Granada, Spain, the summer palace of the ancient Sultans, there is a famous, much copied canal. Long and thin and elegant, it has rows of jets at the sides spraying water hight in the air.

André Le Nôtre, gardener in chief ot the Sun King Louis XIV, who created the gardens for Versailles palace when it was converted from a hunting lodge in the 1660s, was a master at seein water as the ultimate, theatrical flourish. In fact his fountain and canals and lakes used so much water that 14 enormous water wheels had to be built to reroute water from the River Seine. And a new canal, built by 30,000 soldiers, had to take the River Eure all the way to Versailles. But Le Nôtre's greatest effect was a cross-shape canal where the court played on fabulous gondolas. He even commissioned an artifical whale to spout more water jets. This is water as the ultimate design tool.

Arend Jan van der Horst picks out the tried and tested, the stunning plant combinations from his own designs at the Villa Beukenrode in Sassenheim, Holland, to Christopher Lloyd's garden at Great Dixter in Sussex. If you've never seen the round pond at Hidcote, in Gloucestershire, or the square pond at Arley Hall in Cheshire, read on. He takes us through the A-Z of water gardening, the history and the practice, from making formal rectangular ponds to informal ones,

from planting them up with ornamental grasses to the biggest of them all, Gunnera manicata, with leaves the size of a table.

Water gardening is a fun but a specialised art. It does not take long to master, but it needs the help of an expert. Once hooked this could easily become an obsession.

Richard Rosenfeld, East Sussex, 1996.

CHAPTER I

Introduction

Water gardens and plants

Many cultures regard water as the source of all life. In ancient gardens, statues of water gods and goddesses were placed beside the water to emphasize its religious importance; some of these statues have survived or been reconstructed. Neptune, the god of the sea, is the best-known; he is often depicted with his trident, which he used to catch water creatures and fight with seadragons.

Statues have also been used to symbolize rivers and lakes. In the reconstructed garden of Het Loo in the Netherlands, for example, the Ijssel and Rhine rivers are represented by two reclining statues of water gods. And in Cardinal Gambara's fifteenth-century formal garden at the Villa Lante in Italy, water gods are placed on either side of a semicircular waterfall. Often, these reclining statues, resting on one arm, are holding an object with water pouring from it, such as a pot, shell or urn. The male figures often have long, flowing hair and long beards.

As Islam does not allow the depiction of humans and animals, Moorish gardens use ornaments such as pots and bowls instead of statues.

The Renaissance water garden of the Villa Lante

The town of Orvieto, with its beautiful black and white striped marble cathedral, is an essential stop for anyone travelling south from Rome. Nearby is the little town of Bagnaia, with its busy market-place. The garden of Cardinal Gambara, and its two pavilions, were designed by the architect Vignola.

The whole structure of the garden is defined by water, which provides a connecting link between its different features. The garden is located on a wooded hillside, making use of the streams which flow down the hill and also providing a magnificent view of the surrounding area.

Anyone visiting the Cardinal would first have seen a large wall with a deep pool dug at its foot. This pool still contains statues of horses which are sprayed with water by large fountains. You would then continue on to an iron gate in a high wall which, assuming you are welcome, swings open. Behind this lies a long, straight path, to the right of which are two pavilions with the square proportions of Italian Renaissance villas.

Ornaments with water flowing over them, such as this basin, become green if made of porous sandstone. Marble is much more expensive, but does not become discoloured.

Through the gap between these buildings, there is a glimpse of neatly trimmed hedges on a slope and diagonal paths climbing it. Before walking along these paths, you will see the enormous flat garden on the left, divided by box hedges.

At the centre of this garden is a group of statues depicting three boys, perhaps a male version of the Three Graces. They are holding an iron globe representing the world, from which water spouts over their smooth, wet bodies. The drops of water glisten in the sun.

The sculpture is set in a square basin, surrounded by a freestone balustrade and containing stone boat-like ornaments which perhaps symbolize mankind's journey from birth to death.

The box garden is mathematically designed, forming a calming and elegant backdrop to the water-covered statues. There are many paths, and thus many different ways of reaching the centre of the garden.

As you stand in contemplation beside the group of sculptures, you are looking towards the hillside. The two tall and beautifully decorated pavilions on the left and right enclose the flat box parterre. The view between these consists mainly of trees, but there are also glimpses of other man-made features which stimulate your curiosity and provide an incentive to climb the hill.

The water table

The diagonal paths zigzag up the hill between the two pavilions and emerge on a long, flat terrace. At its centre is a large stone table with a channel of fresh, cool water flowing through the middle. This was where the Cardinal and his guests would eat. There were long benches on either side of the table, and the plates, carafes of wine, and glasses were placed on the table. As the food was served, guests could enjoy the fragrance of bouquets of roses on the table.

The guests would have eaten with their hands, and the ready supply of flowing water could be used both to wash their hands and keep the wine cool. The benches, probably made of wood, are no longer there, but the view of the box parterre and the statue of the three boys has not changed.

Looking up the hill, there is another spectacular view of a semicircular bowl with a cascade of water

pouring from it. This has statues of water gods on either side, with long beards and curly hair, and cloths draped round their waists. They are holding urns which have water pouring out of them; this and the water from the cascade falls into two semi-circular basins below.

The water is like a mirror, reflecting the green foliage of the trees, the blue sky, and the white clouds. This area of the garden is full of beautiful little details, such as the stone edging under the basin, which has small fountains spouting upwards from it, each glinting dazzlingly in the sunshine. Around the edges are neatly pruned, centuries-old plane trees, and the grass and topiary hedges form the walls, ceiling, and floor of this outdoor room.

There is a flight of steps leading upwards from

The composition of this statue means that it can be viewed from different directions. Mirrored in the surrounding pond, it becomes even more striking.

behind the two reclining river gods to another dramatic scene: more steps, leading endlessly and steeply upwards. These are a daunting sight, particularly in the heat of summer.

But here again, the water provides relief. The balustrade is a stroke of genius: it has water flowing down it, so that you are never far away from water as you make the long climb, and it is a pleasure rather than an ordeal. The hollowed-out balustrade is at waist height in the middle of the steps so that people can trail their hands in it as they ascend.

At the top of these steps is another large, flat area of

grass, with two beautiful pavilions at one end. These
were used for musical performances, and are linked
by a wall.

When I first visited the Villa Lante twenty years ago,
the guide asked the party to stand on the grass
between the two pavilions. He then disappeared for
a moment, and a few seconds later, much to everyone's amusement, we were sprayed with water from
the roofs of the two buildings. This is an example of
the practical jokes which were already becoming
popular in fifteenth-century gardens.

The area above the pavilions consists of dense
vegetation, which is not accessible. This perfectly
maintained garden is open to the public, but only in
groups accompanied by an Italian-speaking guide.
As a result, it is only possible to spend an hour at

most in this remarkable formal garden. Cardinal
Gambara loved art, and his collection was housed in
the pavilions, where people could talk and eat.

Both of the pavilions in the lower garden are large,
richly ornamented summer-houses with no heating.
They are wholly dominated by the garden; the
central axis is practically enclosed by it. It is unusual
for additional buildings to be placed in a garden in
this way, which is a pity, as the Villa Lante shows
how effective they can be.

The beautiful courtyards and gardens of the Casa Pilatus in Spain show the degree of sophistication achieved by the Moors.

A romantic water garden: Brodick Castle on the Scottish island of Arran

If you have ever visited any of Scotland's castles, you will know that they are just as varied as their southern neighbours. There are Renaissance gardens such as those of Edzell and Kinross castles, semi-formal romantic gardens such as Tyninghame and Crathes, and some magnificent water gardens.

One of these is on the isle of Arran, off the west coast of Scotland just to the south of Glasgow. Arran is a large island of peat moorlands covered in heather and bracken, grazed by sheep and wild horses. There are several little fishing ports, and beautiful sandy beaches. The only disadvantage is the island's high rainfall; this is no Mediterranean resort.

As you arrive on the ferry, you will see Brodick Castle, perched high on the island with exceptional panoramic views. At first sight, the garden might not seem particularly remarkable; it is an attractive Victorian garden with beds of annuals, a rose-covered pergola, and a collection of Mediterranean plants at the highest and driest point of the garden. The Gulf Stream helps to prevent heavy frosts, and

there are many plants here which you would not expect to see growing so far north.

Leaving the Victorian garden, you move into a shady area of mature trees, with the sea always visible. It is here that the garden's crowning glory lies: the large boggy water gardens laid out between the trees.

The ponds are linked by little waterfalls, and this area of the garden is dominated by the sight and sound of running water. It appears to make use of a natural water supply trickling down the hillside, and the peaty soil ensures that the streams never dry out, but this effect can easily be re-created artificially by placing a pump in the lowest pond to circulate the water back up to the top.

At Brodick Castle, the spaces between the ponds are covered in moisture-loving perennials and bog plants. The result is a riot of colours and forms, making this one of the finest water gardens I have ever seen. There are big clumps of blue-leafed *Hosta sieboldiana* 'Elegans', astilbe in shades of scarlet, purple and white, and yellow *Lysimachia punctata*, *Kirengeshoma palmata* and *Alchemilla mollis*. The huge leaves of gunnera give the garden a surprisingly primeval, unreal atmosphere, making it is easy to forget which country it is; after all, gunneras come from the Amazon delta in Brazil.

A few water lilies float in the water, but not so many as to obscure the surface. There are also blue-flowered *Pontederia* and many other bog plants, but I was particularly struck by the fact that there were also so many plants which normally grow in drier soil but will tolerate these conditions; in fact this was one of the reasons for writing this book.

My impressions of the formal garden at the Villa Lante and the romantic water garden of Brodick Castle were very different, but each has a great deal to teach us about the use of water in garden design.

**Overleaf: This pond in Grasse in southern France was
constructed by the Vicomte de Noailles.**

**Here, the cold blue of the pots and pond surround contrasts
superbly with the warm ochre of the building.**

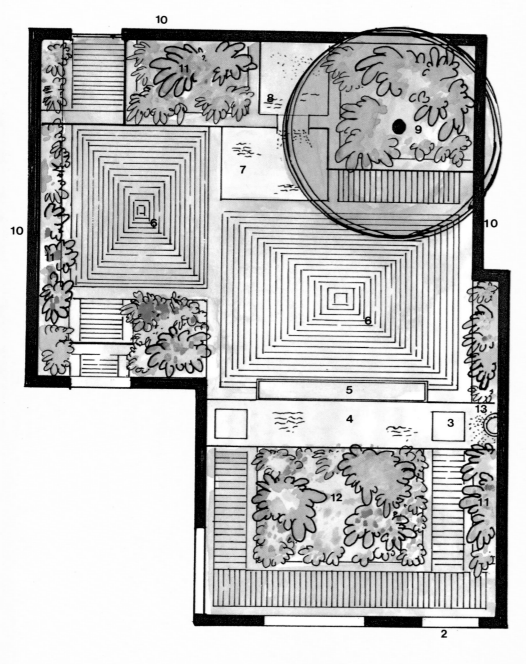

1. living-room with large windows overlooking the garden
2. door to the garden
3. stepping-stone
4. long, narrow pond with brick edging
5. low brick wall for sitting on
6. two brick terraces, the smaller one 30cm (12in) higher than the larger
7. low pond, 15cm (6in) above the large terrace
8. basin 45cm (18in) high, with overflow
9. old dwarf apple tree
10. brick walls, some plastered
11. shade-loving plants: Hosta, Astilbe, Gunnera
12. herbaceous border
13. stone fountain in long pond

Water gardens do not have to contain huge expanses of water if space is limited; the small, enclosed courtyards of Spanish buildings are a case in point. The formal shapes of Moorish garden design, as exemplified in the Alhambra, were my inspiration in the design for a small walled garden, above. The house itself is at the bottom. Coming out through the door, you pass through a low herb garden of rosemary, marjoram, and the colorful *Mentha rotundifolia* 'Variegata'. You then cross a narrow pond using stepping-stones, to a low wall where people can sit and enjoy the garden. The large terrace behind it is given added interest by a raised pond, a waterfall and a basin, with the water circulating between them. The tree is a mature apple which hangs over the brick basins.

CHAPTER 2

The rectangular pond

Different ways of grouping marginal and aquatic plants

There are still some formal ponds in Spain where the water manages to stay clear despite there being virtually no plants. The Moorish conquerors built water gardens all over the country, including the Alhambra palace in southern Spain, which is an example of the Arab tradition of using water in canal-like forms. Most illustrations of gardens from ancient Persia, Turkey or Egypt include formal water features, and it was inevitable that when the Moors landed in Gibraltar in the ninth century they should take this design with them to their new kingdom in Spain.

Many of these gardens were located near mountains or rivers. The Alhambra is close to the Sierra Nevada mountain range, which provides a source of water; pipes and channels were used to transport it to the ponds and fountains of this magnificent palace built for the Moorish sultans.

Many of these formal ponds are located in court-yards, where they glisten like silver mirrors in the harsh sunlight. Some are planted with water lilies; others are empty of plants. One particularly famous example is the Myrtle Courtyard, which centres on a long rectangular pool lined on either side by the myrtle hedges after which it is named. The reflection of the bright green fine-leafed hedge, 1.4m (4ft 6in) high, gives the water a greenish tinge, and because it has no aquatic plants to cover the surface, it has to be kept constantly moving if it is to remain clear.

About half the surface of a pond should be covered by plants. This provides shade which discourages algae growth and protects fish during warm weather.

At one end of the pond is a beautiful round marble bowl, from which a constant stream of cool mountain water wells up and runs down into the pond. At the other end is another bowl containing a tall fountain; the water from this flows invisibly away and reappears in a round basin in the next courtyard.

The Generalife and the long pond

Five minutes' walk away from the Alhambra palace, a private residence was built for the sultan. Its open-plan rooms help to create a cooling breeze, and the whitewashed walls mean that it never gets excessively hot. The Generalife is built on two storeys, with the whole of the ground floor arranged round the inner garden. At its centre is a long, narrow pond with a tiled surround, next to which are very long, spacious flower beds packed full of roses, rosemary, jasmine, and countless other scented flowering plants. The result is a beautiful, fragrant courtyard which is a source of endless surprise and inspiration to everyone that sees it. It is remarkable that so little use is made of these long rectangular ponds in modern-day garden design.

Bodnant Gardens in Wales has a number of spectacular ponds. This very long, highly formal example mirrors the theatricality of the hedges and statues.

Long ponds in post-17th-century baroque gardens

The "grand canal" or long canal became fashionable in baroque gardens, possibly as a result of Dutch influences, not that anyone in France would ever admit this. However it is interesting that canals are so common both in the Dutch landscape and in the baroque garden.

Here, the muted colours of the paving and plants have been designed to create a soothing atmosphere.

But the garden designer André le Nôtre is generally credited as being responsible for the rise of the "grand canal". One of his best-known designs was for the finance minister Nicolas Fouquet, who had a magnificent garden designed and built for his new château at Vaux-le-Vicomte. This has a canal at right angles to the main axis of the garden, and the visitor has to walk round it to reach the statue of Hercules at the end.

At Versailles, which proved to be Le Nôtre's biggest commission, the grand canal was used as a point of termination for an enormously long and wide garden. Everything has been designed to make the long rectangular area of water look even longer.

Wooded areas have been used to narrow the view from the palace, so that all your attention is focused on the length of the canal.

One of the most dramatic features of Versailles, the use of rows of Italian poplars to continue the sightline into the landscape behind, has influenced garden design ever since. This is the water garden at its very finest.

In today's smaller gardens, of course, effects on this scale are not really possible, but a lot can still be learned from them. For example, a long pond can be combined with tall foliage growing on either side and an eye-catching feature placed at the end in order to increase the feeling of length in even the smallest of gardens.

Above and right: I designed this pond in northern Belgium, surrounded by a soft edging of plants including *Rosa* 'The Fairy', *Miscanthus gracillimus* and bergenia.

The long pond in the modern garden

I use long ponds mainly with large numbers of plants along either side. The pure, minimalist lines of the Alhambra's plantless long ponds can look superb in an office atrium or a very modern house, but in a garden full of plants I find that the contrast between the flat surface of the pond and the informal planting beside it is an attractive one. Exactly what this planting comprises will depend on the garden.

Informal planting around a formal pond

Lythrum salicaria, or purple loosestrife, is a wild waterside plant which grows alongside ditches and in bogs and reaches a height of about 1.5m (5ft). When its spikes of violet flowers appear, it makes a strong focal point surrounded by other plants.

Petasites hybridus has round leaves which can be used to fill areas of bare earth along the sides of a pond, but its roots will need to be placed in a plastic container with drainage holes if it is not to become invasive.

Iris pseudoacorus, the yellow flag, seems to be just as happy in the water as beside it, and this plant with its sword-shaped leaves can be placed at intervals around a pond. It flowers early, and therefore does not clash with the *Lythrum*, which is summer-flowering.

Symphytum, or comfrey, is a moisture-loving plant which is also quite happy in drier soils. It has long, broad leaves and usually blue, sometimes pink flowers which mean that it can be used as a strong accent plant.

Another large clump-forming plant is *Eupatorium cannabinum*, which reaches a height of 2m (7ft) and has fairly pale pinkish-red flowers. The fine-leafed,

This pond is in line with the front door, and reached by crossing a carefully tended lawn. *Lavatera olbia* 'Barnsley' is growing against the house.

Here, the plastic pond liner has been covered with wooden edging. A single *Lythrum* 'Morden's Pink' glows in the evening sun, its colour harmonizing with that of *Rosa* 'The Fairy'.

fast-growing meadowsweet, *Filipendula ulmaria*, has clusters of white flowers whose silhouettes make them attractive even when they have died. This is also true of the wild *Hypericum*, which looks superb covered in frost or cobwebs. These are just some of the plants which can be used to form a tall wild border along either side of a pond; of course there are also plenty of low-growing ones for contrast.

Low-growing wild plants

The creeping Jenny or moneywort, *Lysimachia nummularia*, is a wild plant which grows alongside ditches and in bogs. It has yellow flowers and round leaves which make ideal ground cover for damp sites. The wild strawberry, *Fragaria verna*, is another low-growing plant which will spread to cover quite large areas, and the wild lungwort, or *Pulmonaria*, has blue flowers. There are many wild plants such as ivy, veronica and clover which are low-growing. These can be combined with shrubs such as *Rosa rubiginosa*, wild medlar or pollard willow.

Borders of low-growing perennials

Christopher Lloyd's famous garden at Great Dixter, in East Sussex, England, has a formal pond which is

surrounded by an established growth of *Acaena*, which has grown across the flagstones together with *Thymus britannicus* and maiden pink, *Dianthus deltoides*. This is a tried and tested combination grown between stones.

Personally, I would go for rather larger-leafed plants beside a pond, such as *Campanula carpatica* or *C. portenschlagiana*, the large felty leaves of *Alchemilla mollis*, the long-leafed *Pulmonaria*, the fine leaves of low-growing astilbes such as *Astilbe chinensis* 'Pumila', geraniums such as *Geranium sanguineum*, and any suitable flowering or foliage plant reaching a height of not more than 30cm (12in).

There are also low-growing hostas such as *Hosta latifolia* which can be used as ground cover. For a more varied, low-maintenance design, use per-ennials. One easy plant to use in this situation is the masterwort, *Astrantia*; white-flowered forms of this plant include *A. major* and *A. involucrata* 'Haggy'. There are also purple forms including *A. rubra* and *A. major* 'Margery Fish', which flowers for months. For variegated foliage, choose *A. major* 'Sunningdale Variegata'. This has deeply incised leaves, and contrasts well with the round leaves of bergenia, *Rodgersia tabularis*, brunnera or the more elongated leaves of hostas.

You could also combine different plants with similar leaves, such as the incised leaves of acanthus, astilbe

Pink and purple astilbe provide a dramatic backdrop of Victorian pastel colours which contrast with the red water lilies.

and dicentra. Another possibility is a collection of oval-leafed plants such as polygonums, hostas, phlox, euphorbias, and lysimachias. Each of these genuses contains tall and short species. My favourite polygonum is *P. amplexicaule*, of which the pink form, *P.a.* 'Rosea' is even more attractive.

Of the hostas, I particularly like using *H. sieboldiana* 'Elegans' or *H. crispula*. The former has blue leaves, and those of the latter are green with neat white margins. Of the euphorbias, the grey-leafed *Euphorbia wulfenii* is my favourite, while among the lysimachias *L. ephemerum* is a reliable and refined plant. Its three big plus points are its greyish foliage, long flowering period and strong, wind-resistant growth habit.

A green border

In a small garden, you need to be restrained in your choice of colours. One very elegant solution is a border made up of green-flowered plants, such as the green rose, *Rosa viridiflora*, and green hellebores such as *Helleborus corsicus*. These can be grown in combination with some of the many ornamental grasses, such as those with plumes of white flowers, which go extremely well with perennials. One of

these is *Pennisetum compressum*, which reaches a moderate height of about 50cm (20in) and has green panicles with attractive purple bristles. The hardy green grasses include *Molina altissima*, *Stipa pinnata* 'Gigantea', which reaches a height of 2m (6ft 6in) and the many species of miscanthus.

Ornamental grasses can be extremely effective. Many American gardens are made up of nothing but large groups of low-growing grasses combined with small groups of taller ones. It is important to grow grasses in drifts so that the garden does not look too much of a jumble.

The effect created by grasses growing alongside water and waving in the breeze is a magical one, and they have the added attraction of golden yellow foliage in the autumn. Grasses should be cut right back in the spring to encourage new growth.

Roses by the water: the Villa Beukenrode

There are many gardens in Spain and Italy which show how well roses and water go together. This is not a combination which normally springs to mind, as roses are associated with hot, dry positions. However, they can look particularly good in this situation, perhaps grown with a range of perennial plants, provided you are restrained in your choice of colours. I discovered this when I designed a garden for the Villa Beukenrode in the Dutch town of Sassenheim, where I combined roses with perennials alongside a water feature. My brief was to turn a large area of meadow behind this art deco house into an ornamental garden. To entice the owners out into this garden, I designed a large, long pond which served as an eye-catcher. One side of this was laid to grass, and along the other side was a wide border of yellow and white flowering plants: achilleas with their tall yellow heads of flowers, ligularias, white phlox, and white spring anemones. These were interplanted with white and yellow roses: the large-flowered *Rosa* 'Peace', the vigorous white *R.* 'Schneewittchen' and the brilliant yellow *R.* 'Allgold'. The result was a very eye-catching display, despite being located a considerable distance away from the patio of the house.

Right: The calm and stillness of a simple rectangular pond on a hot summer's day.

These plants were combined with the ornamental grass *Miscanthus sinensis* 'Gracillimus', which forms large, attractive clumps of arching stems, and the smaller tuft-forming grass *Pennisetum compressum*. These look good in winter, particularly with the addition of the single bamboo which I placed right at the end of the pond. I chose *Sinarundinaria murielae*, which has to be kept carefully in check to stop it spreading.

Behind the pond, I placed a terrace with a pergola over it. There was space left around the border and the terrace for a wide shrub border, combining species roses with evergreen pines. The garden already contained one gigantic pine, probably *Pinus radiata*, and I planted several much younger ones which have already reached a height of 6m (20ft).

Behind the shrub border is a beech hedge, which turns brown in the autumn. In winter, there is a striking combination of colours: a brown hedge and many different shades of green in the form of the pines, the bamboo, ground-covering plants, and grass. The pond is an endless source of fascination all year round.

Cobbles and concrete edging give a Mediterranean feel to these two interlinked ponds, with a splash of colour provided by the Japanese flag, *Iris kaempferi*.

Recent additions

A garden is a living thing which evolves all the time. Since I finished this one, the owners have placed a beautiful statue of a young woman's torso in front of the ornamental grass, *Miscanthus sinensis* 'Gracillimus'. A number of *Chamaecyparis lawsoniana* have also been placed alongside the path between

A subtle blend of purple loosestrife (*Lythrum salicaria*) and the brown seed heads of *Typha latifolia*.

the border and the hedge; their distinctive shape helps to give the garden a structure in winter. These have been underplanted with the evergreen creeping perennial, *Pachysandra terminalis*.

In and around the pond

The pond, with its dancing fountain, has achieved a perfect ecological balance. It has deep-water and floating aquatic plants such as the water soldier, *Stratiotes aloides*. Water lilies float on the surface, but there is also plenty of space left uncovered to offer a view of the depths beneath, including the fish. These, unfortunately, provide tempting prey for the heron which visits on a daily basis. I also placed blocks of peat around the edges of the pond. These are still used as fuel in some countries, and I placed them so that the earth behind them was slightly higher than the blocks themselves. As a result, the

blocks are in contact with the water, which keeps them damp and makes them an ideal growing medium for many moisture-loving plants such as lady's mantle, campanula, lysimachia and ferns. One additional benefit was that because the peat blocks consisted of rotted vegetation, they were full of wild plant seeds such as heather, rushes and hypericum. Over the years, these have grown into an attractive mat of vegetation.

Bog plants in a long rectangular pond

If you want to be able to stand at one end of a long pond and see its full length, there are a number of different ways in which you might plant it. One possibility is to have narrow planted borders along

Unmistakably autumnal shades of brown, yellow and green. The plant in the middle is *Ligularia dentata* 'Desdemona', whose leaves have purple undersides.

the two long sides, with a slightly wider strip of bog plants at the end. To emphasize the length of the pond, you could use tall, thin, hardy bog plants.

One such plant is *Typha angustifolia*, which is narrow, upright, and grows to a height of 2m (6ft 6in). It has distinctive cigar-shaped seed heads. *Scirpus* or club-rush is another upright plant, though it has a tendency to droop slightly at the top. There is also a variegated variety, *S. tabernaemontani* 'Zebrianus'.

For flowers, try *Ranunculus lingua grandiflora*, which grows to a height of 1m (3ft) and has saucer-shaped yellow flowers over a long period in summer. This needs to be kept in check if it is not to become invasive.

You can also create tall vertical accents at the ends of the pond as well as the sides. This will decrease the feeling of length by creating a flimsy curtain of greenery, but has the advantage that you can sit behind it and look through it at the water.

Right: *Ceanothus arbutus* **'Cascade' needs a sunny, sheltered position. Wisteria makes a more hardy substitute in colder climates.**

Red and yellow can be an overpowering combination, but here, against a background of greenery and elegant architecture, it works perfectly.

The round forms of the water lilies, ligularia and polygonum contrast with the straight lines of the tree trunks and the pond.

This Italian-style pond is set against a backdrop of green hedging, using a very architectural, minimalist approach.

Vertical and round forms: a dramatic contrast

You can create contrasts with these tall vertical plants by juxtaposing them with the round leaves of kingcup (*Caltha palustris*), bog arum (*Calla palustris*), or other plants with oval leaves such as *Alisma aquatica*. Pickerel weed (*Pontederia cordata*) has blue flowers, and there is also a white-flowered variety, *P.c.* 'Alba'. The arrowhead (*Sagittaria japonica*) also has leaves of this kind, as does *Houttuynia*, with more or less heart-shaped leaves and insignificant cone-shaped flowers, each surrounded by four white bracts. *Lysichiton*, the skunk cabbage, has white or yellow flowers and huge oval leaves up to 1m (3ft) long, so it is not suitable for the sides of the pond, but would look good at the end. You should experiment with different forms and combinations until you find one which harmonizes with the other plants in the garden.

If you have used many spreading plants along the edges of the water, such as hostas, campanulas and geraniums, do not place tall plants immediately beside them in the water. Treat the planting in and beside the water as a single entity, and if necessary do a rough sketch to give yourself an idea of what the forms will look like next to one another before you plant them, as this will avoid jarring contrasts.

Floating on the water

When people think of ponds, the first plants which usually spring to mind are water lilies. These have highly attractive foliage, and flowers ranging from copper, salmon pink, and yellow through to red, pink, purple, and white. Try matching the colour of the water lilies to that of the surrounding plants. If you have pink plants growing beside the pond, try planting a pink water lily such as *Nymphaea* 'Marliacea Rosea', or better still the purple *N.* 'Attraction'. If you have yellow-flowering plants around the pond, try *N.* 'Sunrise'.

Apart from the water lily, perhaps the best-known plants with floating leaves are the members of the pond lily genus, *Nuphar*, such as *N. minima* and *N. lutea*. These have the advantage of tolerating moving water and light shade, both of which are a problem for water lilies. Another popular plant of this kind is the frogbit, *Hydrocharis morsusranae*, a plant which has white flowers resembling a very small water lily. Unlike many other floaters, it is not

invasive, though its plantlets will gradually spread to form a mass if they are not detached.

Making rectangular ponds

A rectangular pond can be made fairly economically using a flexible pond liner. Because you do not want to have to replace it in five years' time, the liner's resistance to ultraviolet light is an important practical consideration.

Start by using stakes to mark out the shape of the pond in accordance with the design, and then begin the excavation. If using certain kinds of pond liner, you will need to send the design to the supplier so that they can cut the liner to shape for you. In this case, you will need to dig a hole whose shape and size is as close as possible to that in the drawing. Other liners can normally be bought off the roll or in fixed sizes, and can then be folded to form the corners. Wood is one material which is easy to use in building the edges of rectangular ponds. If the pond is small, a wooden beam around the rim will do; if the sides are longer than 2m (6ft 6in), the timber will need to be anchored every 50–60cm (20–24in) using vertical pegs. Choose new wood which has not been treated with non-oil-based materials, so as not to contaminate the water. Untreated and soft wood rots quickly and is therefore not a good idea. It is very important that the liner should not be visible once the pond has been filled with water. How you ensure this will depend on the design of the pond. You can also use different methods in one pond, for example by having a steep timbered bank on one side, and a flatter side where the liner is covered with pond soil and plants. In some cases, such as in Japanese gardens, the liner can also be covered with gravel and pebbles of various sizes. You should also make sure that the soil in the pond is not in contact with that outside it, as this can create a siphon effect. If you use gravel as a covering, the chances of this occurring are minimal.

The Italian pond on Sir Osbert Sitwell's estate at Renishaw in Yorkshire. The 'isolotto', or little island, conveys the idea of solitary contemplation.

Water as an extension of the house
Right: My brief here was to brighten up a house and garden with a distinctly gloomy feel to them. The garden was dominated by trees, with large conifers excluding the light. I designed a garden with the emphasis on cheerfulness, using water to create a bright, open feeling along with beds of white roses and herbaceous perennials. The sombre conifers had to go. Fortunately, I managed to persuade the owner that these drastic changes were necessary. The huge living-room window gave a dramatic view of the garden, and the pond was therefore aligned with this, and surrounded by lady's mantle and hostas. A yew hedge was planted at the far end of this relatively short area, with a Lutyens bench in front of it. The flower beds contained fragrant roses and many grey-leafed and white-flowered plants. With a white sun umbrella and white cushions on the bench, the garden became a warm and sunny-looking place, and gradually turned into an extension of the house.

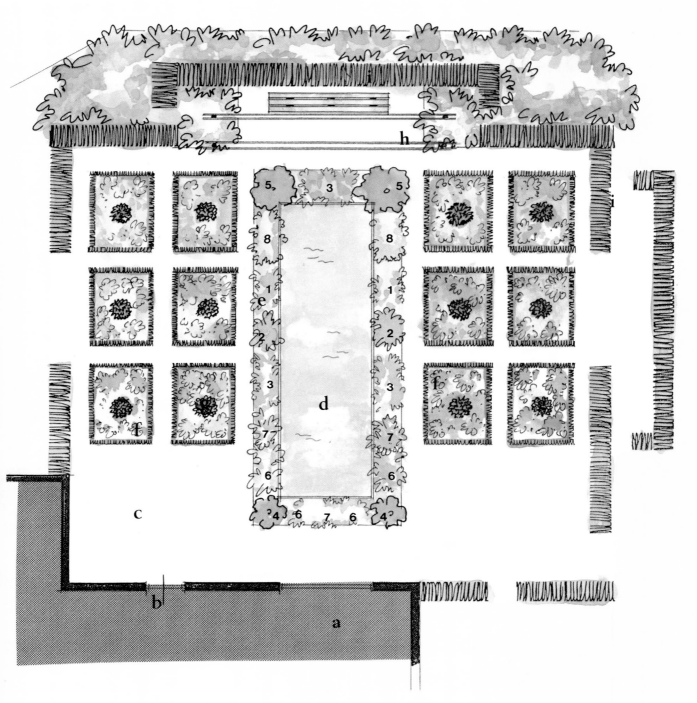

a living-room with large window	**1** *Alchemilla mollis*
b back door	**2** *Hosta crispula*
c patios	**3** *Polystichum setiferum*
d long pond	**4** *Skimmia japonica* 'Foremanii'
e lady's mantle	**5** *Enkianthus campanulatus*
f beds of white-flowered perennials	**6** *Rodgersia podophylla*
g beeches pruned into obelisks	**7** *Hosta fortunei* 'Hyacinthina'
h pergola	**8** *Anemone* 'Honorine Jobert'
i yew hedge	

CHAPTER 3

Round ponds

From classic grandeur to total informality

Round ponds were widely used in classical gardens. They were usually located at the intersection of two or more paths, or at intervals along a path or avenue. One of the greatest examples of such avenues is at Versailles, where a flat area behind the palace is laid out with large ponds, lawns, flower-beds, and broad paths. Then comes a round, shallow raised pond containing a flight of stone steps, on which stand statues of frogs, spouting water. At the top of the steps is a magnificent statue of a woman.

This is followed by a grass avenue with broad paths along either side of it, which in turn are lined with woodlands of chestnuts and other trees. The next landmark on the walk round the gardens is a huge round pond containing statues of water gods on horseback.

This is one extreme, but a round pond can also make a distinctive centrepiece for the smallest of gardens, perhaps with a circular or rectangular stone surround. One possibility is to build one raised basin inside another, with the water pouring down from one to the other. This arrangement is particularly common in Mediterranean towns and gardens.

An old-fashioned rose bush helps to soften the outlines of this formal circular pond.

It has a long historical pedigree; in Moorish Spain, for example, waterfalls and fountains were widely used to please the ears as well as the eyes of visitors to a garden. The Moors built many raised stone ponds, a sturdy and elegant form of ornamentation which was imitated for centuries afterwards.

But even before the time of the Moors, the Egyptians, Mesopotamians, and other civilizations had produced complex systems of conducting water so that it spouted upwards or tumbled over the edge of a raised pond. They were also aware of what happens when a tank is filled with water to a certain level and linked by a pipe to a lower pool containing a fountain of about the same height as the tank. For a fountain to work effectively, its base needs to be 1m (3ft) or more below the level of the tank.

Here, upright plant forms have been used to contrast with the round leaves of the water lilies.

Stadholder William III of the Netherlands used this system when he had a garden built for himself and his wife Queen Mary II at their hunting lodge in Apeldoorn. He created a tall fountain by building reservoirs filled from natural streams, which were then connected to a pond in a sunken garden about 15m (50ft) below the reservoirs. This fountain was built to commemorate William's coronation as king of England in 1689.

If you want a constantly spouting fountain in your garden, you will need a natural or artificial water supply which raises water to a level high enough to create a fountain of the height you require. Of course there are other options available, such as electrically operated pumps, if you do not have a natural source of water pressure.

Round ponds in Lisbon

Large gardens need a readily available source of water, and in Lisbon's botanical garden this has been provided in the form of raised circular ponds, which have been made into a feature of the garden in the same way as flower-beds. The ponds are strategically positioned along the main path, and at every point where it is intersected by another path.

Each pond is surrounded by a wide variety of old-fashioned fragrant roses. The gardens are full of mature palms and other trees, and the many exotic plants which thrive in this warm, dry climate.

The round pond at Hampton Court

One of the most distinguished gardens in Europe is that of Hampton Court, the magnificent Tudor residence of the British royal family until the eighteenth century. It was built on the banks of the Thames by Cardinal Wolsey and given to Henry VIII, who enlarged the buildings.

The palace then remained largely unchanged for two centuries, until William III and Mary II came to the throne in 1689. William made a number of major alterations; another huge edifice was built on to the rear of the palace, with a courtyard between the two. The façades of the new building were designed by William and Mary's famous architect, Sir Christopher Wren. The courtyard is now grassed over, and there is a round pond with stone edging in the middle of the lawn. A fountain spouts high into the air, and the water shimmers in the sunlight as it descends. When I was there, the deep blue sky and vivid green grass made the garden into a powerfully beautiful work of abstract art.

Left: *Iris pseudacorus variegatus* **dramatically breaks the harmony of round plant forms. This pond has been designed to look like a section of river.**

Below: This is actually a circular pond which has been given a completely informal shape by careful planting.

The combination of delicate roses and the hard, moss-covered stone of the pond surround creates an extraordinary feeling of tranquillity.

Round ponds

A circle is a self-contained form which in itself cannot be used to create a sense of direction. If you want the appearance of a round pond to change as you look at it from different angles, you will need to create contrasts between tall plants and low-growing ones, perhaps leaving some areas unplanted.

Imagine you are looking at a garden from a patio, with a round pond just in front of you.

To increase the feeling of distance, you could place taller plants on either side of the pond, and leave the middle unplanted. Alternatively, if you wanted to foreshorten the garden and reduce the sense of distance, you might place tall plants at the ends of the pond. Use similar tall, thin plants to those you would use for a long rectangular pond, such as *Typha*, *Scirpus* (club-rush), and water buttercup, and try to visualize the arrangement in your mind before you actually plant them, with the emphasis on contrasting forms.

Choosing aquatic plants for a round pond

Do not allow the surface of your pond to become completely covered in water lilies or other aquatics, as you will then lose the effect of the water glistening in the sun. Water lilies should therefore be planted in plastic baskets of heavy loam to prevent them from spreading too far. To create circles of water lilies with plenty of space between them which will let the water show through, place the baskets 2m (6ft 6in) apart. Water lilies look particularly good when combined with a tall group of club-rush or *Typha*.

The same is true of the brandy bottle, *Nuphar lutea*, which again needs to be grown in a container to restrict its growth. Where space is limited, use smaller versions of these plants, such as the water lily *Nymphaea pygmaea*, and the yellow pond lily *Nuphar minima* 'Variegata'.

A majestic fountain in the distance can make an eye-catching focal point for a garden.

When I designed this long pond, I placed identical benches at either end. The grass also provides a connecting link between the plants.

You will also need oxygenators beneath the surface of the water, such as *Ceratophyllum demersum* (hornwort), *Elodea canadensis* (Canadian pond-weed), *Hippurus vulgaris* (mare's-tail), or *Hottonia palustris* (water violet). The latter has pale lavender flowers and is one of the few flowering oxygenators. Other good oxygenators include *Potamogeton crispus* (curled pondweed), which has feathery leaves, and *P. natans*, with oval leaves.

What to plant around the outside of a circular pond

One relatively small garden which I designed in the centre of Amsterdam was dominated by a huge circular pond 5m (16ft) in diameter. This had a patio of flagstones around a part of its circumference, and flower beds around the rest. The beds were relatively.

narrow, so that they could be tended from the flagstones alongside them. There was a strong accent in the form of an ornamental rhubarb, *Rheum tanguticum*, on the left-hand side viewed from the patio and the house. This contrasted with the fine, upright long leaves of *Iris sibirica* and the heart-shaped foliage of brunnera. Aquilegia, ferns, lady's mantle, and ajuga were also distributed around the outside of the pond together with spring anemones, bergenia, and some evergreen shrub ivy. The result was dreamlike and informal, and met the need for variety combined with low maintenance.

A symmetrically planted pond edge

At the Villa Beukenrode in the Dutch town of Sassenheim, I designed a round pond in the front garden, which previously consisted of grass, trees, and shrubs. The pond was positioned right outside the front door, like a mirror. Behind it, I planted two *Miscanthus sinensis* 'Gracillimus', which formed broad, arching clumps. That was all that was needed

by way of planting, though I also placed two lead herons in the pond, and a patch of pond lilies creating a simple but very eye-catching result.

Another garden I designed in the town of Eext, also in the Netherlands, was based on two very different ponds. One was a long rectangle surrounded by a symmetrical arrangement of gunnera, lady's mantle, and other plants which looked good beside water but tolerated relatively dry conditions. I planted the other large pond, which had already been built using a plastic liner, solely with wild flowers. I arranged these asymmetrically around the pond, giving brief glimpses of the water from the house and other vantage-points in the garden.

A pond surrounded by perennials

At Hatfield House in Hertfordshire, England, the Marchioness of Salisbury has created a magnificent pond garden. The pond is surrounded by yellow *Rosa* 'Golden Wings', with a great variety of other hardy flowering perennials such as erigeron, lady's

Left: A feast for all the senses; the sandy, ochre-coloured stone forms an attractive background to fragrant roses and a quietly playing fountain.

The garden which Anthony Paul created for himself is a sumptuous and distinctive blend of oriental features.

In this nature garden, the small pond was designed as a source of drinking water for birds and other creatures.

Myosotis palustris, the water forget-me-not, creates a lacy fringe of blue around a slightly murky-looking pond.

mantle, and campanula. The plants create a gently swaying screen around the pond, which is kept in constant motion by a fountain, and the air is filled with the sound of trickling water.

A round pond with ivy

I once saw a courtyard garden in Paris which was unusually large for a city where land is so expensive. This had a large round pond set in an area of gravel, which was bordered in turn by trellises on three sides, the house being on the fourth side. The trellises were covered in fast-growing climbers such as Virginia creeper and ivy. Ivy was also planted around the edges of the pond, and it looked superb. It created a shiny evergreen border for the pond, and the owners let it spread randomly outwards from the pond leaving patches of bare gravel between the foliage.

Cast-iron chairs and a large wrought-iron table were the only other forms of ornamentation in this almost maintenance-free garden.

The round pond at Knightshayes

In parts of south-west England, the normally gentle English landscape becomes harsh, forbidding, and awe-inspiring. There are many good gardens to visit here, with hedges, mature trees, and enormous rhododendrons being used to shelter them from the wind. One example is the enormous garden at Knightshayes, near Tiverton in Devon, which is really more of a park than a garden.

The first sight is of undulating hills and ancient oaks, and then there is a sunken rhododendron garden with many unusual colour combinations. Next comes the formal garden, made up of hedges, grass, urns, and a pond garden. If you walk through the garden quickly, you can very easily miss the pond altogether; it is surrounded by a tall and dramatic yew hedge which has been sculpted into crenellations, like those of a castle. The enclosed garden itself is laid to lawn, with the circular pond at its centre and a statue of a goddess behind it. Beside the statue is a grey-leafed ornamental pear tree, *Pyrus salicifolia*. There is nothing else in this extraordinarily tranquil

A combination of tall marginals and water lilies helps to keep the sun off the water and thus to keep it clear.

Filipendula rubra is a perennial with feathery plumes of very small pink flowers.

and beautiful little space, but it repays many visits. Its minimalist, cleverly topiarized hedge is a source of inspiration, and the unusual trees lurking beyond the hedge, behind the sculpture and the pear tree, are a reminder of the fascinating botanical specimens outside. The pond area is a place to rest for a while before exploring the wonderful collection of plants which lies beyond.

The garden proper is an enormous woodland area with lawns, twisting paths, and a huge variety of shrubs, conifers, ornamental grasses, perennials, ferns, and bulbs. Knightshayes is a garden for all tastes and all seasons.

The round pond at Dumbarton Oaks

In 1921, the American diplomat Robert Woods Bliss bought a plot of land planted with beautiful trees in the fashionable area of Georgetown, near Washington, DC. Here, he and his wife built a garden containing areas of different styles, reflecting the gardens which had influenced them during their long stay in Europe. Working with the garden designer Beatrix Farrand, they began by building an imposing house, which is now a museum. This stands on a hill with the garden sloping away on all sides. There are a number of elegant baroque pond gardens, paved with black and white patterns of tiles.

The garden has two interesting round ponds. The first is in a sunken area, reached via a long flight of steps. At the bottom of these is an area of grass, surrounded by a ring of lime trees and a formal hedge. Grass is the only form of ground cover. At the centre of this space is a large circular pond with a stone ornament in the water.

The atmosphere is calm and contemplative, and this area was inspired by the monastery garden, where a fountain or well was often the sole form of decoration in a courtyard enclosed by cloisters.

Here, the long broad leaves of *Lysichiton* and other plants have been used to soften the edges of a rectangular pond.

The garden at Dumbarton Oaks is a compilation of features which Mr and Mrs Bliss had seen in European gardens. Their Lovers' Lane, for example, is inspired by the Arcadian Academy in Rome, and is enclosed by a living fence of bamboo. There is also an open-air theatre, with the seats consisting of steps cut into the side of a hill.

Beatrix Farrand made models of various parts of the garden, and these were then sent from America to London, where Bliss was the US Ambassador. His wife also had a major influence on the overall design. Eventually the couple decided to establish a foundation, which now owns what is quite possibly the world's largest collection of gardening books and designs, attracting academics from every corner of the globe.

Japanese iris, *Iris kaempferi*, should be kept dry in winter to prevent the leaves being damaged by ice. *Carex stricta* 'Bowles variety' is an evergreen, tuft-forming sedge.

Arums need to be kept covered in winter, or kept in a cold frame.

If you ever visit Washington, I definitely recommend setting some time aside to visit the monastery garden, the Lovers' Lane, and the pond garden of Dumbarton Oaks. They provide a reminder that ponds do not necessarily have to be surrounded by flowering plants, and that they can be used as sculptural features in their own right, mirroring the beauty of the surrounding garden.

The round pond at the Villa Reale

The Villa Reale is a privately owned garden in Lucca, near Pisa. The formal villa is used by its owners, the Italian Prince Pecci Blunt and his wife, to receive guests in summer. When they are not in residence, the garden is open to visitors.

Napoleon's sister Elisa Baciocchi removed most of the formal garden in front of the house when she became ruler of the principality of Lucca. She had the hedges demolished and the sculptures moved to create a beautiful landscaped park. There are still

Right: The ostrich or shuttlecock fern, *Matteuccia struthiopteris*, likes damp conditions and makes a good architectural plant.

some reminders of the formal garden which once stood here, in the form of a large pond and a small collection of sculptures. This area is laid to grass, which is left unmown in summer and is therefore filled with wild flowers.

Fortunately, Elisa did not change the formal Renaissance section of the garden, which is out of sight of the house. This is now home to an outdoor theatre surrounded by cypress hedges. In front of the hedges stand life-size terracotta figures of Pulchinello and Columbine, and in summer recitals, plays, and operas are performed here.

The walk to the theatre, along a shady lane lined with sunlit lawns and wild flowers, takes you through two interesting gardens. The first is through an iron gate, which leads into a slightly gloomy area

Choosing one particular style of plant helps to create a sense of unity amid variety. Here, the scene is dominated by feathery astilbes, which lead the eye to the water.

surrounded by tall laurel hedges. At its centre, a bright splash of light is created by a circular pond with a dancing fountain in the middle. The area is paved with plain tiles, and dominated by the sight and sound of water; the effect is stunning. Keep going, and you will come to a square pond surrounded by stone balustrades; there are always two white swans swimming here when I visit.

Lemon trees in pots are arranged round the pond and along a side path leading on to other gardens; the elegant statues of water gods are the dominant feature of the water garden. Your walk then takes you through a copse to the outdoor theatre.

The Villa Reale is a fine example of how varied Italian Renaissance gardens can be. Water is regarded as an important sculptural element which forms a centrepiece for the entire garden.

The round pond at Hidcote Manor

Sometimes it is difficult to see whether a pond is actually round or oval; one such example is at Hidcote Manor in the Cotswolds. This garden is divided into different sections with admirable artistic flair; designing a garden on a sloping site with so many changes in height, deep valleys, and streams, was no easy task.

Lawrence Johnston was not content simply to design an English landscaped garden on several levels;

The gunnera, which comes from Brazil, has the largest leaves of any temperate garden plant.

instead he took advantage of the differences in height to create a truly beautiful garden.

The main avenue lined with borders of pink and red flowers leads outwards from the house, with other paths and compartments leading off the sides to many different types of garden. One of these is a fuchsia garden, which marks the beginning of the red borders. The first stage in the walk round the garden is an enclosed courtyard with a path through the middle and begonias and fuchsias in delicate shades of pink on either side.

After this area, two topiary birds made from yew form a gate through which the distant sound of water can be heard. As the visitor walks through the gate, all is revealed: a large, round and extraordinarily blue pond comes into view. There is only one path round it, which leads to a fountain in the shape of a dolphin and a boy.

This waterfall looks like a completely natural feature, but it is very much a man-made creation. The cracks in the wall would be an ideal place to plant ferns.

Exactly in line with the previous gate is another one, again made of topiary and this time taking the form of a tympanum, or triangular panel, above a gap in a tall, dense yew hedge which leads further into the garden. The pond itself is unusual, in that it is difficult to establish its precise shape without measuring it.

A ready-made pond in the Netherlands

Some old farmhouses have slurry pits which fall into disuse when the cowsheds are no longer used to house animals. These can be put to good use in a garden, as can be seen at the Huis de Dohm, in Heerlen in the south-eastern Netherlands. This had a concrete pit beside the coach-house which was originally used to store horse manure.

When the current owner and her husband moved into the house, it was clear that the coach-house would be used for other than its original purpose. Eventually, it became an exhibition hall, garden ornament shop, and café for groups visiting the garden.

The slurry pit behind this building was overlooked by huge windows, and was very unattractive. The logical thing to do was to fill it with water and make it into a pond, edged with rounded stone slabs which covered the edge of the pit. A yellow and white garden was then planted around the pond, and surrounded by a yew hedge. This garden combines yellow lilies and daylilies, yellow perennial *Viola cornuta*, lady's mantle, and syringa. The result is an undulating border of interesting plant forms around the large pond, which itself is planted with a few lemon-yellow water lilies, yellow irises, water buttercups and marsh marigolds. Apart from the water garden, this constantly changing creation has many borders, arbours, a marvellous vegetable garden, and a wild-flower garden.

Left: A hilly site is not necessarily a disadvantage when designing a garden; working on different levels, with water flowing from one to the other, can add extra interest.

Right: Here, a neatly curved area of lawn has been cleverly used to create a "bridge" between two separate ponds.

The round pond in an Amsterdam city garden

A circular pond is such a self-contained shape that it does not detract from its surroundings in any way, and can therefore be used just about anywhere. Sometimes, I will choose a circle precisely because it will not dominate the rest of the garden.

When I was asked to design a garden for a beautiful late nineteenth-century house in the centre of Amsterdam, I began by drawing a circle. The garden was actually much too small for such an imposing, richly decorated house, but it needed a sense of grandeur to counterbalance the architecture, which is why I designed a circular pond 5m (16ft) in diameter. Immediately outside the house there is an elegant flagstone patio which adjoins the edge of the pond,

Steps down to the water may be a place to fish from, or simply somewhere from which to gaze into the depths of the water.

so that the square tiles contrast sharply with the rounded pond. Around the rest of the pond are delicate plants which reduce the feeling of grandeur to more manageable proportions, and a few large-leafed plants such as *Rheum tanguticum*.

Lamium, achillea, ferns, lady's mantle and the tall blue-flowered *Iris sibirica* were planted round the edge of the pond. In summer, the planting is dominated by the round leaves of *Hosta crispula*, which are green with white margins. In winter, the greenery is provided by the low-growing shrub ivy, which is planted on one side of the flagstone patio, and by camellia 1m (3ft) high on the side of the water, which is protected by reed matting against severe frosts.

The simplest and most attractive way to conceal the edges of a pond liner is to cover it with plants.

Beside the camellia, a spiral staircase leads up to the balcony, giving a view over the garden. I installed a tall fountain so that it is visible over the railings of the balcony as soon as you come into the first-floor living-room. This gives a foretaste of the garden down below and encourages people to come out of the living-room and look at it.

Right: The pond in the front garden of this house catches the light as you come out through the front door, and therefore required a minimum of planting around its edges. Two clumps of the ornamental reed, *Miscanthus sinensis* 'Gracillimus', were placed as accent plants at the back of the pond, so that the light falls between them and is reflected on the surface of the water. Behind the pond is a beech hedge lined with holly, hazel, and oak trees. As the house is slightly higher than the garden, there is a good view of the pond, which means that its small size is not a disadvantage. However the rules of perspective mean that the further a pond is away from you, the less you can see of its surface; this is something to bear in mind when deciding how large a pond needs to be.

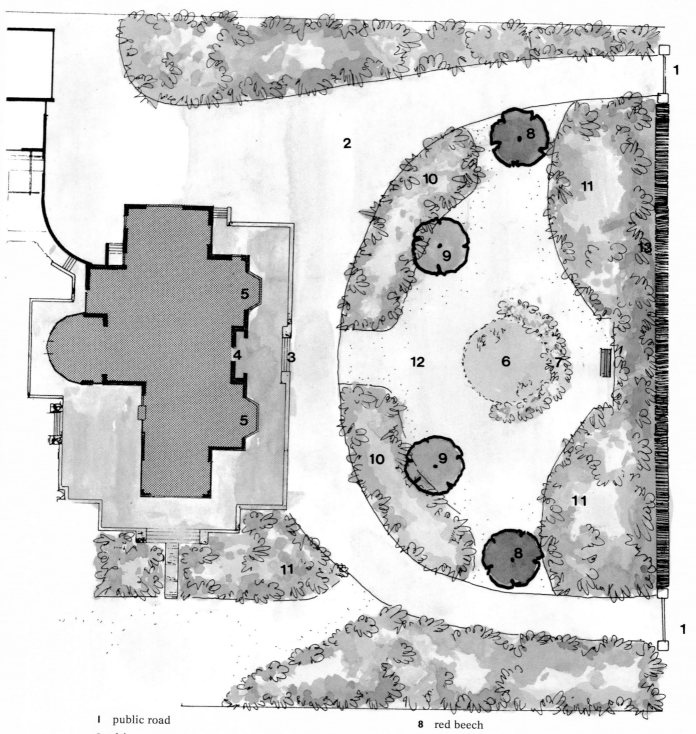

1 public road
2 drive to garage and house
3 steps to patio surrounding house
4 front door
5 living-room and study
6 round pond
7 ornamental grasses: *M. Sinensis* 'Gracillimus'

8 red beech
9 white-flowered *Prunus*
10 mixed shrubs
11 evergreen planting
12 grass
13 hedge

CHAPTER 4

Square ponds

The square as a self-contained shape

Rectangular and oval ponds increase the sense of distance, but round and square ones do not. Why is this?

Imagine a path with rows of trees on either side. The trees create a strong sense of perspective; because they recede into the distance, they invite you to follow the path and find out where it leads to. This is something which artists have discovered in painting and drawing; perspective is a powerful medium which can be used to advantage. The trees beside the path look big when you look sideways at them, but if the path is long, those at the end are reduced to dots in the distance. Objects a long way away look smaller than those nearby.

This was why Renaissance and baroque gardens began to favour long ponds over round or square ones. People wanted to explore the world that lay outside the narrow confines of their household, town, or even their country. The long pond was a reminder of infinity, and came to symbolize a break with the established order. Round and square ponds reflected an acceptance of the structures within which people lived, such as families, churches, and guilds. The square and the circle were safe, self-contained worlds, offering peace, simplicity, and compliance, which were important virtues in earlier societies.

In a raised pond, the plants and animal life are easier to see. A box hedge has been grown around this pond to cover the large area of bare brick.

The square as focal point

In ancient Islamic gardens, circular, square, and octagonal ponds were used as the central features of courtyards. All of these are mathematical, self-contained forms which are perfectly symmetrical.

These gardens were divided into paved and planted areas. If they contained ponds, which they usually did, these would be edged with tiles made of marble, local stone, or fired clay bricks.

Where the garden had flowers in it, there would still be a stone border between the flower-beds and the water. The idea was to emphasize the lines of the pond and flower-bed rather than to let them flow into each other. Gardens were filled with fragrant, brightly coloured flowers, their appearance changing

Blocks of peat laid round the edges of a pond absorb moisture and become covered in moss and plants. They can look superb if properly laid and maintained.

from hour to hour and from season to season. Fragrance and colour were particularly important, and fountains were almost essential.

The fact that square ponds also appear in Islamic gardens shows that sometimes a quiet focal point in an enclosed courtyard was preferable to a long, dramatic pond.

The square pond at Arley Hall

Late nineteenth- and twentieth-century English gardens often use square ponds as the centrepiece of a garden enclosed by hedges or walls. In this respect, they bear a close similarity to the old Islamic pond gardens, but there are also major differences. In England, the pond is usually surrounded by a large area of grass, with evergreen shrubs such as box, yew, or rosemary pruned into spheres. The grass may be broken up by narrow flower borders and flagstone paths, often placed immediately around the edge of the pond. One very good example of this layout is in the garden of Arley Hall in Cheshire.

Here, a very large, symmetrically divided garden is surrounded by yew hedges, with more mature yew trees dotted around the area. These stand on the

The concrete edges of this pond are not particularly attractive, but the weathered bricks and fountain provide a visual distraction.

The same pond as that on the previous page, part of a harmonious composition of green foliage, pink roses, blue lavender, and old brick.

edge of a large sunken garden which is about 40cm (16in) below the rest of the garden. The two are separated by low stone walls overgrown with rockery plants such as alyssum, dianthus (pinks) and saponaria.

A small lead figure of a child stands on a pedestal in the middle of the square central pond; this reduces the garden to a more human scale and makes it calming rather than overwhelming. The effect would have been completely different if a stone or lead statue of a warlike Diana or Hercules had been used instead. Flagstones have been laid around the pond and the front path, and the understated reddish colour of the stone makes a perfect combination with the grass.

Arley Hall, located not far from Manchester, has one of Britain's oldest and most imposing border

gardens. It dates back to 1835, when two broad areas of grassland were dug up, leaving a wide grass path in the middle. Both sides of this path are now red brick walls; behind the right-hand wall is a vegetable garden, and behind the one on the left is a series of themed gardens.

The grass between the walls on either side of the central path was then removed, and what may have been the first-ever flower borders were planted in 1835. These are still there in all their glory; they are

As the years have passed, parts of the brick edging of this pond have become completely covered by lady's mantle and other plants.

The angled position of this pond, together with the planted areas and hedge, focus attention on the next part of the garden.

at least 100m (325ft) long, and are broken up into compartments by placing long yew hedges against the walls. At the end is an arbour, which makes a very effective eye-catcher.

A square pond in Belgium

One of the more surprising discoveries I have made in my travels is the very high quality of some Belgian garden design. Many of the best gardens are attached to large villas, converted farmhouses, and castles, and are not normally open to the public.

One enthusiastic owner showed me round her own large private garden, which she had redesigned after being inspired by some of the gardens she had visited with me. It is a woodland garden which receives little sun, and huge drifts of hostas, astilbe, rodgersia, and other shade-loving decorative foliage plants have been planted under the trees to create a wonderful environment.

The most recent change was the removal of a cut-flower garden, which was replaced by a pond area paved with brick and tiles. This long strip of land formerly housed a plastic tunnel used for growing

flowers, which has now been replaced by a square pond. There are paths leading to the pond, with gulleys designed to lead rainwater into it, and it is surrounded by blue and white perennials, roses and annuals. The garden also has hedges around the outside, creating a strong architectural feel with the square pond as the focal point.

Two ponds at one of Belgium's top restaurants

Het Laurierblad is one of Belgium's leading restaurants. It recently became a hotel as well, and its rather dull lawn had to be converted into a proper landscaped garden, with the grass being removed and replaced by stone paths and patios for the guests to stroll around.

When I designed the garden, I tried to create close visual links between the restaurant indoors and the garden outside.

I did this by building a long, rectangular pond which was overlooked from inside, and placing patios on either side of this mirror-like, eye-catching feature. For extra effect, and so as to create movement in the water, I designed a square raised pond with stone

walls at the far end. The water from the raised pond flowed into the rectangular one via a waterfall, which meant that a system was needed to pump the water back up into the raised pond. I did this using four stone columns placed beside the raised pond; the water flowed up through these. The result was a hypnotically fascinating spectacle which lured the restaurant's customers out on to the terrace for a stroll and a drink.

Continuing the theme of cooking and eating, the area round the pond and terraces was made into a herb garden. Because the garden was off-centre to the restaurant, there was space for a path which will eventually be covered over with a canopy of apples and pears. The herbs and fruit are there fresh for the picking, providing a source of inspiration for the

In certain situations, a purely horizontal composition with neat edges and almost no verticals can be very effective.

chef and pleasure for the guests who flock to the garden.

The combination of a square raised pond and a rectangular one was technically complex, and I had to bring in a specialist builder and architect, but the result was a success.

Pre-formed square ponds

Sometimes, an owner will want their garden to have a water feature, not want it to be dominated by a large pond. I therefore sometimes use pre-formed square ponds which can be dug into position beside a patio, path, or flower-bed. These have wide shelves on which troughs, pots or baskets of aquatic plants can be placed.

The ideal depth is about 70cm (30in), deep enough for a water lily to be placed in a basket on the bottom and survive the winter. I often place peat blocks around the edge of the pond and then allow plants such as achillea, ferns, or periwinkle to grow over the side. If the owner needs to be able to reach the water's edge easily, I use tiles or bricks to conceal the unattractive plastic rim.

This woven willow screen provides shelter from the wind, and can be removed in summer to provide a view of the fields beyond.

When I built a small pond in my own garden, I planted large-leafed trailing ivy to cover the rim and trained it so that it now provides a thick covering of shiny evergreen foliage which is attractive all year round.

There are really no limits to what you can plant round such a pond, and the fact that it is so symmetrical need not be a deterrent; you can soften the outline using perennials, shrubs, and topiary. As you enjoy the tranquillity of the pond and the way in which it contrasts with the plants, you will realize why one of the basic tenets of garden design is that the ideal garden should combine relaxation with tension, and predictability with surprise.

Exploiting the symmetry of square ponds

There are many different situations to which a square pond is suited. The most obvious is as the centre point of a traditional flower garden, with the pond being surrounded first by a gravel, tiled, or brick path, and then by beds or borders. The flower-beds might contain roses, perennials, or herbs, and the whole of the garden can be made into a self-

The pottery jars apparently scattered at random above this little hidden pond are in fact a carefully arranged composition.

Old railway sleepers or ties have been used as the edging for this huge square pond.

contained entity by the addition of a hedge. The second possibility is to install a square pond beside a patio as an eye-catcher, and place a wide variety of decorative foliage plants around it. This works very well, provided the edges of the pond are properly concealed using tiles, wood, turf, and/or plants; this is important, because the pond is designed to be viewed from close up, and any imperfections are therefore very apparent.

The third possible position for a square pond is at the far end of a grass path, with a few distinctively shaped aquatic plants in it. One suitable candidate is the tall, hardy reedmace *Typha angustifolia*; alternatively, you could use large-leafed water lilies, whose foliage and flowers provide a dramatic backdrop to a grass path.

One drawback of square ponds is that they need to be seen from fairly close up; if viewed from a

distance, they look narrower and rectangular. If the pond is too far away from a viewpoint, a rectangular one may therefore be more suitable.

Place a few tall accent plants behind the pond, and plenty of attractive foliage plants hanging over the side. Bergenia is a good choice; another is the tuft-forming ornamental grass *Pennisetum compressum*, which looks attractive until well into winter, and the round or oval leaflets of *Epimedium* make good ground cover. Alternatively, use evergreen ferns; there are not many to choose from, but three particularly attractive examples are *Phyllitis scolopendrium*, the hart's-tongue fern; *Polystichum munitum*, the giant holly fern; and *Blechnum capense*. You should also include a few plants with a more rounded growth habit to contrast with the square shape of the pond. These might include a clump-forming evergreen bamboo such as *Sinarundinaria murielae*, rhododendrons, box pruned into topiary spheres, and the shrub ivy *Hedera* 'Arborescens'.

Try also to plant something delicate-looking beside the pond to soften its outlines. You might use an ornamental grass such as *Molina altissima*, or a hardy shrub like *Enkianthus campanulatus*, *Nandina*

Container-grown plants enable the layout of a pond to be altered to suit changing seasons and personal whims.

This pond, and the pots at the end, are carefully designed to lead the eye into the next section of the garden behind the hedges.

domestica or *Nothofagus antarctica*. The vigorous *Rosa moyesii*, with its bottle-shaped hips in the autumn, would look good; so would white standard roses. At the front of the pond, where the plants need to be low-growing, try grass, periwinkle, or ivy.

The informal pond

There are many situations where square, rectangular, and round ponds are simply not suitable because a more natural look is required. At Brodick Castle on the Scottish island of Arran, for example, the water garden has such an abundance of vegetation that there is not a straight line or symmetrical form to be seen anywhere. Irregular shapes are often more appropriate in large gardens and rural environments than in small, rectangular suburban gardens, and not everyone has the knack of making these artificial creations look like natural features. The Royal Horticultural Society's garden at Wisley in Surrey, and the Savill Garden near Windsor, are two examples of leading gardens containing informal ponds. These have provided inspiration to countless visitors, and features such as waterfalls, streams, and narrow, irregularly shaped ponds have become a common sight in urban gardens as a result. At their worst, these look totally out of place, but at their best, if they are designed with a sense of proportion and use plenty of foliage plants, they can look absolutely irresistible.

A plain, natural lake

The Serpentine, in London's Hyde Park, lives up to its name; it is a long, winding lake which takes a good hour and a half to walk round. It has little inlets, bridges, boathouses, and trees, but there are few marginal plants and most of the lake is surrounded by grass. The Serpentine is a fine example of how beautiful a large area of water can be on its own, without any additional features.

Right: In this design, the house is at the top and the back door leads out on to a series of paved areas. To introduce some variety into this rather narrow section of the garden, I installed a 1.5m (5ft) square pre-formed pond, surrounded by lady's mantle, hostas, and bamboo. I also used Waldsteinia ternata, a low-growing, spreading, yellow-flowered evergreen with strawberry-like leaves, in places which were to be left more open to ensure that the water was visible from the patios. The hostas and lady's mantle were not planted in the line of sight, as they were too tall.

The pergola creates a certain amount of shade, which makes the light-reflecting properties of the pond even more important.

When planting a pond, consider what it will look like in winter. Here, evergreens such as ivy have been used to ensure that the pond will not lose its allure even in the depths of winter.

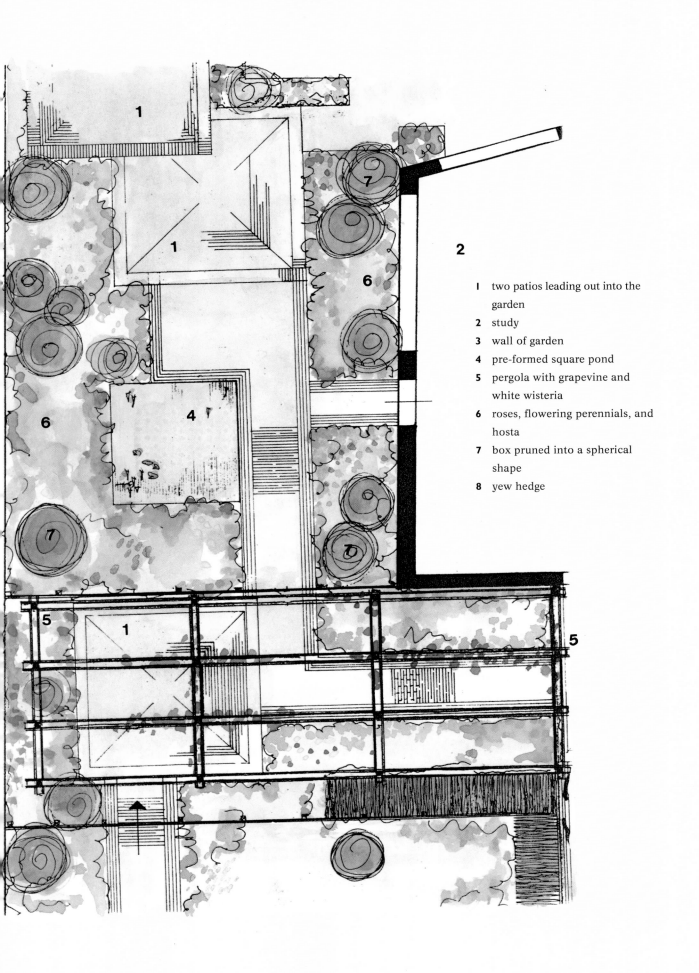

1 two patios leading out into the garden
2 study
3 wall of garden
4 pre-formed square pond
5 pergola with grapevine and white wisteria
6 roses, flowering perennials, and hosta
7 box pruned into a spherical shape
8 yew hedge

CHAPTER 5

Plants for damp locations

A waterside composition using ornamental grasses of various heights

Some gardens in North America are planted with ornamental grasses and nothing else, and the effect can be very striking indeed. In nature, large areas of sand-dunes are often covered by marram and other grasses which wave to and fro at the slightest breath of wind; this effect can be re-created even in a very small garden, using ornamental grasses such as *Pennisetum*.

As well as creating this soft, wavy effect, many grasses turn golden yellow in autumn and stay that way until the early spring. They are then cut down to give the new, fresh green shoots plenty of room to grow. *Pennisetum* does not have the feathery panicles of other grasses; instead they are bristly and arching, turning from green to purple and then to ochre in the autumn.

Many grasses look good beside water because they strengthen the impression of dampness and lush growth. *Pennisetum* is one example, but the shiny leaves of *Miscanthus* are even better in this situation. There are many species and varieties; one is *M. sinensis* 'Strictus', which reaches a height of 1.5m (5ft) and has stiff, upright glossy leaves with yellow stripes. My favourite of all grasses is *M. sinensis* 'Gracillimus', which I have recommended elsewhere in this book. It has attractive, broadly arching stems which reach a height of about 1.75m (5ft 9in).

Primula pulverulenta is one of the candelabra group of primulas. It flowers in late spring and looks superb alongside a pond; there are also orange and white varieties.

Apart from *Miscanthus*, other grasses such as *Festuca*, *Helictotrichon*, and *Panicum* also have beautiful stems. If you are as keen on grasses as I am, you will find many different ways of using them close to a pond. They form an ideal point of transition between wet and dry soil, as they will thrive in both.

Large-leafed plants

The most dramatic large-leafed plant is the gunnera, a bog plant from Brazil which looks superb beside a pond. In ideal conditions, and if the roots are able to reach water even in dry summers, the plant will reach a maximum height of around 2m (6ft 6in). Its slightly crinkly leaves and long, scaly flowers give

Pennisetum alopecuroides forms a round tuft and has beautiful panicles of flowers in late summer.

It is not immediately apparent that there is a pond here at all, which is potentially hazardous if there are children about. Here, the tall stems of *Miscanthus japonicus* have been used for vertical emphasis.

the plant a primeval, almost other-worldly look which can be used with dramatic effect.

Gunnera must be used carefully, because not all other plants go well with it, and in a small garden where the aim is to create an understated, delicate effect, gunnera is way over the top. Instead, use something more subtle such as *Alchemilla mollis*, *Geranium endressii*, or hostas, with their large numbers of oval leaves. Low-growing ground-cover plants that like damp conditions and provide a counterweight to large, dramatic plants include *Lysimachia nummularia*, *Dicentra*, and *Vinca*.

The round, layered leaves of *Hosta sieboldiana* 'Elegans' have an almost sculptural feel beside this pond.

Another large-leafed plant which is suited to damp conditions is *Rheum palmatum-tanguticum*, the ornamental rhubarb. This has attractive incised leaves and a tall plume of purple or pink flowers which are not everyone's idea of beauty.

Rheum palmatum is the common rhubarb, which has white plumes of flowers and goes well in cottage gardens. Its large leaves need to be contrasted with another plant, such as the sword-like foliage of *Iris sibirica*, which also likes damp soil and has white, blue, lilac, or pink flowers, or the round or oval leaves of plants such as the clump-forming *Polygonum bistorta*. This is a member of a large genus which also includes the Russian vine.

Polygonum bistorta is a very vigorous plant which has become semi-naturalized in many countries. It has a base of oval leaves with long stems bearing spikes of small pink cylindrical flowers which last for a long time. After the plant has flowered, the attractive foliage lasts until winter.

A white-flowered group to go beside a pond

One attractive small to medium-sized plant to grow in boggy conditions is *Lysimachia clethroides*, the Chinese loosestrife. This has very small white flowers and lance-shaped leaves, and reaches a height of about 60cm (24in). Another white-flowered plant for this situation is *Astilbe* 'Deutschland', which reaches a height of 70cm (30in) and has feathery plumes containing many small flowers; two similar varieties are 'Gladstone' and 'Professor Van der Wielen'. The trio can be completed by the white-flowered *Hosta undulata*, with its bright green leaves and white leaf stalks and bracts.

Knap Hill and Exbury azaleas come in many bright and soft tints. The variety 'Sylphides' is a soft pink, here combined with ferns and hostas and arching downwards to the water.

Right: In this project, I was asked to turn the fields beside an old farmhouse into ornamental gardens which could be used by an art gallery to display sculpture. The owner of the gallery wanted the area to include a wide variety of garden environments.

I started by placing a large granite-tiled courtyard immediately outside the farmhouse, marking the starting-point for an exploration of the garden. From here, a long pergola leads to the rest of the garden, which is divided into compartments. Visitors can wander round the small lake or visit the greenhouse full of pot plants, and there is also a beehive surrounded by plants which attract bees.

The area round the lake is planted with hortensias and many different large-leafed plants such as petasites, *Peltiphyllum peltatum*, and gunnera, the largest of the temperate foliage plants.

The edges of the lake are planted with ivy and periwinkle so that they look attractive even in winter. Visitors can wander round looking at the sculptures, which are set amid avenues of willows, apple trees, and tall Buddleia.

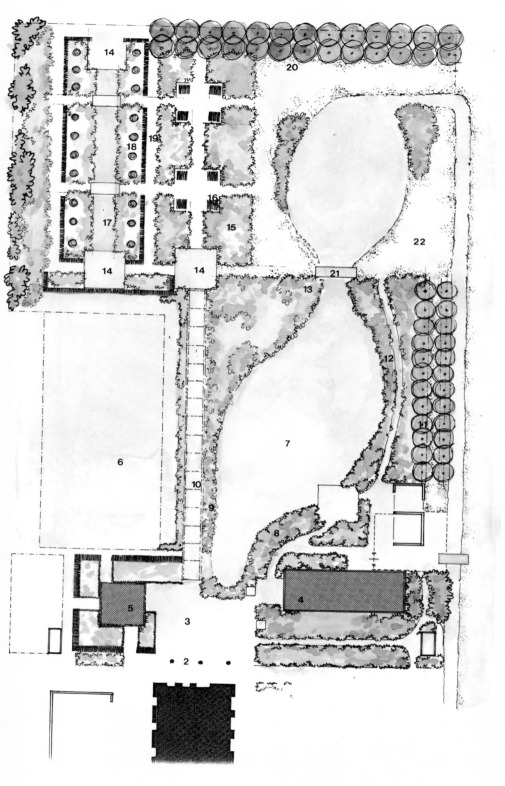

1   house and art gallery
2   three mature lime trees
3   large brick patio
4   greenhouse containing pot plants and sculptures
5   cast-iron arbour, 7m (23ft) high, with white wisteria
6   tennis court
7   new lake
8   foliage plants
9   *Hortensia* varieties
10   cast-iron arched pergola with ivy, roses and honeysuckle
11   willows and petasites
12   large-leafed plants: gunnera, rheum, and hosta
13   sun- and moisture-loving plants: iris, bergenia, and pennisetum
14   square terraces used to display sculptures
15   yellow-, white-, and blue-flowered perennials and roses
16   cubes of box
17   long rectangular pond
18   ivy and apple trees
19   beech hedge
20   avenue of pear trees
21   bridge
22   lawn

CHAPTER 6

Maintaining the ecological balance of a pond

Why plants are so important in a pond

Plants produce oxygen, which is essential both to plant and animal life. All aquatic and bog plants release oxygen into the environment; the more sunlight they receive, the more they produce.

Fish and other pond animals are dependent on the oxygen in the water, and at nights, when there is less of it available, they rest so that they consume less. It is therefore important that your pond should contain plants whose leaves grow underwater, so that their oxygen is released directly into the pond.

Below: The attractive round leaves and seed pods of the lotus flower.

Right: *Orontium aquaticum* has unusual pencil-shaped flower spikes.

How much oxygen is present will depend on the water temperature; warm water contains relatively little, and the oxygen content increases as the temperature falls. When water is just above freezing, it contains an average of 14.2mg of oxygen per litre of water; at 10°C (50°F) the oxygen content falls to 10.9 mg per litre, and at 20°C (68°F) it is 8.8mg.

Extra oxygen is therefore often necessary in warm weather. You can add this using an underwater pump which releases bubbles of air into the water, or you can keep topping up the pond with a hose. But the best way of dealing with this problem is to install a fountain or water spout of some kind, consisting either of a short piece of tubing or a more elaborate ornamental fountain. This has the twofold benefit of oxygenating the water and creating the sound of running water. In still water, only the 5cm (2in) or so

A stroke of inspiration: wisteria trailing down towards a pond. Growing in the water is the Cape pondweed or water hawthorn, *Aponogeton distachyus*.

Large groups of *Lysimachia punctata* look particularly good beside a pond.

nearest the surface contains oxygen. Pouring water into the pond creates movement and forces the oxygen deeper into the water; wind can also do this to a certain extent.

What else plants need to produce oxygen

Plants die if they are deprived of light, but in normal circumstances they convert the sun's energy into organic matter by using the cells in their chlorophyll to produce sugar molecules. Apart from sunlight, the production of these molecules also requires water and carbon dioxide; the latter is produced by animals. So plants and animals are interdependent; animals need oxygen, and plants require carbon dioxide.

Plant waste products

Books about gardening often refer to the acidity or alkalinity of garden soil or pond water. This is measured using pH; if water is very alkaline, it has a high pH, and if it is very acidic, its pH is low. A scale from 0 to 14 is used, with 7 being neutral; the ideal pH for a pond is between 6.5 and 8.5.

As plants die and decay, they increase the acidity of the water. They also give off ammonia, a gas which

dissolves easily in water to form ammonium hydroxide. Ammonia is harmful to plants and fish even in small concentrations, and the more acidic the water, the greater its ammonia content will be.

It is therefore very important that the level of plant waste should be kept to a minimum, particularly in ponds which are closed systems and where the water is only renewed periodically.

Fortunately, this ammonia is converted into harmless nitrite by a water-dwelling bacterium called *Nitrosoma*. This plays an important part in keeping the pond healthy, and like all organisms it needs a properly oxygenated environment. Its ideal habitat is a layer of gravel on the bottom of the pond.

Bacteria multiply rapidly in water with a high oxygen content, and can sometimes use up quite a high

Covering large parts of the water with plants, in this case water lilies, helps to keep the sun off it and thus prevents algae growth.

proportion of the available oxygen, so they may also be one of the reasons why there is not enough of it in the pond. As a result, the balance of the pond must be maintained using a combination of oxygenating plants, moving water, and possibly a submerged air pump. If your pond is situated near trees, it will also need a net placed over it in the autumn in order to prevent dead leaves from falling in, sinking to the bottom, and decaying.

The pretty yellow flowers of *Nymphoides peltata* growing on the pond are echoed by the daylilies in the background. Also floating on the pond is *Nymphaea laydekeri* 'Purpurata'.

are more likely to leach into the water. If this is the case, you may need to dig a drainage channel alongside the pond to prevent it from happening.

Your pond may also be contaminated by groundwater seeping into the pond from peaty soil, which will make it too acidic, or by lime from concrete paving, making it too alkaline. Both problems can be remedied using a pH buffering agent, available from garden centres. If your water is too alkaline, you may also have to repaint concrete surfaces with pond paint.

Finally, even small quantities of paints and wood preservers can wreak havoc if allowed to drip into the water. Take appropriate precautions when applying these to fences or garden furniture near the pond, and always use non-toxic preservatives in preference to corrosive creosote.

As mentioned earlier, fish have difficulty breathing in warm water. Your pond will therefore also need to include a reasonably deep section where the temperature does not fluctuate too much, and where you can plant deep-water aquatics to shade the surface. Shallow ponds may be easier to construct, but they are more trouble than they are worth.

Avoiding pollution from outside the pond

Another factor you should consider when designing your pond is the possibility that the surrounding soil may have been contaminated by chemicals such as weedkillers or artificial fertilizers. This is particularly important if the pond is on a slope, as the chemicals

Left: The theme of the pond can be continued elsewhere in the garden, with moisture-loving plants grown in pots and other containers.

This kind of controlled jungle effect, with gunnera as the centrepiece, is suited only to larger ponds. The plants need to be prevented from spreading too much and becoming untidy.

Green water and blanket weed

Green water is largely an aesthetic problem; it does not mean that conditions in the pond are unhealthy. It is caused by huge numbers of microscopic algae floating in the water.

These algae grow when there is plenty of sunlight, and are particularly prevalent in the spring, so the best solution is to shade the surface of the pond. If you have water lilies and other deep-water and floating aquatic plants, they will do this job for you; you simply need to be patient and wait for them to spread until they cover a reasonable area of the pond. Ideally, about half of the water surface should be covered.

It is possible that your pond may remain stubbornly green even though you have plenty of plant cover on the surface. There are various remedies available, including placing bales of barley straw in the pond or using chemical algicides. These are often effective, but will need to be repeated every few months.

Blanket weed is another type of algae, consisting of long green threads which float in the water and attach themselves to the sides of the pond. If allowed

This bench has been carefully positioned for maximum enjoyment of the sights and sounds of the pond.

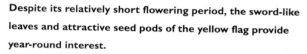

Despite its relatively short flowering period, the sword-like leaves and attractive seed pods of the yellow flag provide year-round interest.

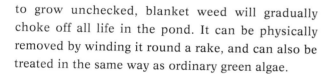

There are numerous different forms of the Japanese flag, *Iris kaempferi*, with white, pink, purple, and blue flowers. The sword-like leaves can be used to create contrasts with other plants.

to grow unchecked, blanket weed will gradually choke off all life in the pond. It can be physically removed by winding it round a rake, and can also be treated in the same way as ordinary green algae.

Dirty water

Brown, muddy water is another problem which is mainly aesthetic; it does not do any particular harm to the plants and animals in the pond. It may be caused by soil leaking out of the tops or sides of planting baskets, or you may be using a pump which is too powerful. Usually, it is fairly easily dealt with; baskets can be protected by lining them with hessian or a similar material, and by placing a layer of gravel over the top.

Sometimes, though, more drastic action may be needed. If too thick a layer of silt has built up at the bottom of the pond, it may need to be emptied and thoroughly cleaned. This is a laborious job, which is why prevention is better than cure; if you keep a close eye on the pond throughout the year, and deal with problems such as fallen leaves before they become too serious, a complete overhaul will not be needed very often.

Nevertheless, no matter how good the environmental balance in your pond may be, you will find that silt will inevitably form at the bottom. Some leaves will always slip through the net, and plants in the pond will also decay.

When you clean your pond, start by lowering the water to a level where the fish will be easier to catch, and place them in a container, making sure that the temperature of the water is the same as that of the pond. When you have finished, float the container in the pond for 15 minutes or so until the temperatures have equalized, and then release the fish.

Using filters to maintain the ecological balance

Many ponds manage quite happily without a filter to
keep the water free of algae and waste products.
However, it may be necessary to install one if you are
having trouble keeping it clear despite following the
instructions given above, and it is essential if you are
keeping koi or other large fish which tend to stir up
the sediment on the bottom of the pond.

Mechanical filtration

There are two ways of filtering water: mechanical
and biological. A mechanical filter pumps the water
through a container filled with a filtration medium
such as sand, gravel or foam granules, which strain
out the algae and particles of dirt.

Lythrum salicaria **has spikes of violet flowers from
midsummer to early autumn, and is sometimes found in
boggy locations in the wild.**

This is the simpler and less expensive option; at its
most basic, it may consist of a block of foam placed
over the strainer of the pump, though there is some
doubt as to the effectiveness of this measure. A
mechanical filtration system may be located inside or
outside the pond, and the outlet pipe may be used to
operate a waterfall or fountain.

Biological filtration

The other more complex and expensive option is biological filtration, which essentially uses a colony of bacteria to break down waste products and toxic ammonia. Here, the filter unit is placed outside the pond, just above or below the level of the pond, with the water either falling or being pumped into it. The filtered water then goes back into the pond, usually in the form of a waterfall.

This system is particularly suited to larger ponds, where it does not dominate the pond visually and it does not matter where the filters are located. Unlike a mechanical filtration system it needs to be operated continuously, or the bacteria will die. The filter chamber can be concealed with plants so that it looks like another small pool.

Fountains

I believe that a fountain is an almost essential ingredient of a formal pond. Firstly, it creates the sound of moving water, which has a curiously pleasant and relaxing effect on the human mind.

Secondly, the fountain helps to keep the water properly oxygenated, particularly in warm, still summer weather.

Bear in mind that a fountain is an artificial creation which does not occur in nature, and will therefore look out of place in an informal or wildlife pond; it is also generally agreed that a fountain should not be used in combination with a waterfall, because the two create a visually cluttered effect.

When siting your fountain, make sure that it is kept well away from water lilies, as even small quantities of spray can seriously damage them. Also, make sure that it is in scale with its surroundings, with the spray no higher than about half the width of the pond, and that its style is appropriate to that of the pond and the rest of the garden. A statue of a cherub spouting water into the air will almost certainly look out of place in the more modern formal pond in a town garden.

The fine leaves of *Scirpus lacustris* 'Albescens' glow a deep golden yellow in the sun. For variegated leaves, choose *Acorus calamus* 'Variegatus', the myrtle flag or sweet flag, which has the added bonus of tangerine-scented leaves.

Osmunda regalis, the royal fern, certainly lives up to its name. It makes a stately centrepiece, particularly when its tall brown flower spikes appear.

Acer palmatum is commonly used in Japanese gardens for its finely incised leaves which turn red and yellow in autumn. *Acer palmatum* 'Atropurpureum' has reddish-purple leaves throughout the summer, turning bright red in autumn.

Right: Every cloud has a silver lining; this house near Zierikzee, on the Dutch coast, suddenly acquired a lake after a dyke collapsed.

I designed the back garden so that the main focus was on the lake, using hedges to break it up into more manageable units, each with its own character. The garden is full of herbaceous perennials and roses, which are reflected in the reed-fringed lake.

There was already one weeping willow growing beside the lake, and I planted another to frame the surface of the water, surrounded by large groups of hostas and gunneras.

Finally, I built a little jetty where the owners could fish, contemplate the beauties of nature, and decide how they were to keep the rapidly-spreading reeds in check.

Choosing a pump

There are two main types of pump used to operate fountains, depending on the height of the spray to be created. Submersible pumps are used in smaller ponds, and are simply laid on bricks on the bottom of the pond. The pump is connected to the fountain head by a length of flexible plastic pipe. The smaller pumps, giving a spray up to about 1.2m (4ft) high, use a low voltage and are therefore safe to install yourself; otherwise, have your pump fitted by an electrician.

Surface-type pumps are far more powerful and expensive than submersible ones, and are installed in specially constructed housings or chambers outside the pond. They draw water from the pond through a plastic hose, and discharge it to the fountain through another one. You are only likely to need such a pump if you want a particularly large fountain, or if you wish to have a more complex feature, perhaps involving the operation of several fountains at the same time.

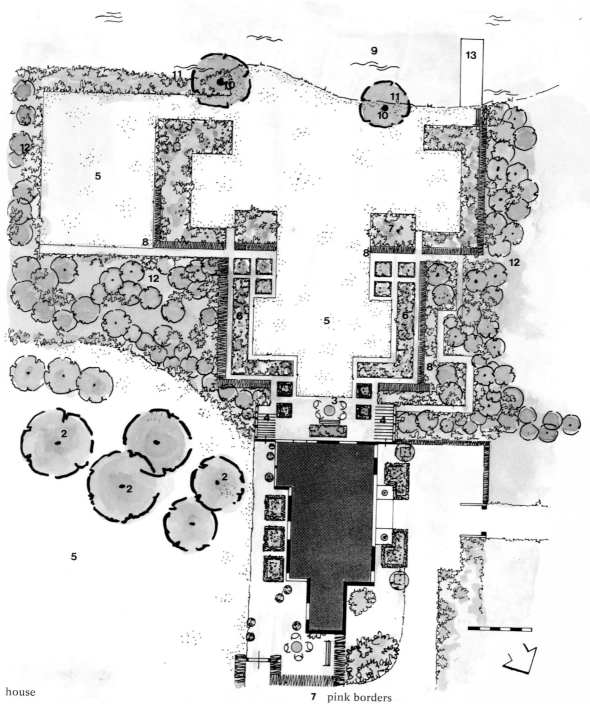

1 house
2 mature chestnut trees
3 terrace
4 two pergolas covered in roses and clematis
    for shade
5 lawn
6 blue, white, and grey herbaceous borders

7 pink borders
8 yew hedges
9 lake
10 two weeping willows
11 gunnera
12 flowering shrubs and trees
13 jetty

CHAPTER 7

Building ponds and swimming-pools

Important things to remember when building a pond

In the past, ponds were built from puddled clay; the wet clay was slapped on to the sides of the hole and then smoothed down with a spade. It was important that the clay was always under water once the pond was built; if the water level fell and the clay was exposed to the sun, it would quickly dry out and crack, causing the pond to leak. Keeping the pond filled must have been a constant chore, though planting moisture-loving plants around the edges to shade them from sun would have made the job somewhat easier.

Puddled clay ponds are few and far between these days. They are still sometimes built in nature reserves and on areas of heathland and woodland where the soil is constantly wet. They make an ideal home for amphibians and other wildlife, and it is still sometimes possible to obtain subsidies to build clay ponds if they are of environmental importance.

Small children and water are not compatible, so a pond needs some kind of protection until the children have learned to swim. Use a material which is not too conspicuous, such as chicken-wire.

The bottom of the pond

Some pond owners are lucky enough to have a pond full of fresh, clean, natural water rather than one filled from a tap. Not long ago, I dug a pond on my own farm in the Netherlands. The contractor who excavated it could not go too deep because the water in the peat underneath the clay topsoil was brackish. The pond was partly intended to provide an important source of drinking water for the sheep that grazed in a fenced-off meadow on the far side of the pond, so it would have been useless if the water had been undrinkable.

My pond, which is now full of natural groundwater, shows how complicated a process excavation can sometimes be. Many garden owners find that the groundwater is either too deep, or that its level fluctuates too drastically. Both of these situations can occur if you live in an agricultural area where the groundwater has been pumped away to improve the drainage for crops.

If the water is some way below ground level, you can compensate for this by creating a gentle slope downwards from the house, so that the surface of the water is visible from the house or patio.

A flagstone or tile edging can look a little hard when it is first laid, but after a few years it will have become smothered in plant growth.

Most of us, of course, do not have the luxury of large amounts of space and a natural water supply. As a result, the great majority of ponds nowadays are built using pond liners.

Choosing a pond liner

The best and most expensive material for a pond liner is butyl rubber, which will last for decades. It is not damaged by ultra-violet rays or frost, and is a very flexible material. It can also be welded or glued together where you need a pond liner which is larger than the width of the roll.

A less costly option is PVC, which is not so durable but will still last you for perhaps 15 years. The best PVC liners cost only slightly less than butyl, and incorporate a web of terylene which makes them

It is still possible to obtain old stone horse-troughs, which make excellent water features.

much more durable. Unlike butyl, which is black, PVC comes in a variety of colours, but avoid the temptation to choose anything other than black or perhaps brown.

If you are not confident about welding or gluing strips of butyl together, have this done by a specialist. If the pond is not too large, it may be best to stick the strips together in order to form the shape of the pond first, so that it then simply has to be unrolled into a hole which has been dug to exactly the right size.

Excavating the pond

The process of digging a hole for a pond is not as simple as it sounds, and needs careful planning. Start by tracing out the shape of the pond on the ground, using a garden hose, a piece of rope or a line of sand. This will give you a clear idea of how the pond fits in with its surroundings. A pond should not be less than about 60cm (24in) deep; this will give plenty of room for deep-water aquatic plants and for fish and other animals. You will also need a shelf about 15–20cm (6–8in) deep and 30cm (12in) wide, around all or part of the pond, on which to place baskets of marginal plants.

It is very important to ensure that the edges of the pond are perfectly horizontal, as otherwise the surface of the water will be out of true. Use a spirit level on a board to ensure that this is the case.

Before you install the liner, remove any stones or other objects which might puncture it, and place a protective layer of sand, old pieces of carpet or newspaper in the hole.

A pond liner must be carefully installed; if this is done less than perfectly, it may develop leaks. Place it over the hole so that there is plenty of overlap round the sides, and weight it down with bricks or other objects. Then fill the pond using a hose, moving the weights as the liner settles into the hole, and trim the surplus material so that there is an overlap of about 15cm (6in) all round.

Your next job is to cover the edges of the pond liner. There are various ways of doing this, most common of which is to use paving stones, laid on a mortar mix of three parts sand to one part cement and extending about 5cm (2in) over the edge of the water. Other possible materials include brick, wooden boards, and turf; the latter has the advantage that you can have greenery right up to the water's edge.

Pre-formed pools

These used to be a poor second best to flexible liners, but their quality has improved greatly in recent years. They come in a wide variety of shapes and sizes, and may be the best solution if you want something which is relatively small and simple to install. In addition, they are often the best way of creating a raised pond, particularly as they take the weight of the water off the walls of the pond.

The cheaper varieties are made of vacuum-moulded plastic, and are often semi-rigid. They tend to deteriorate quite rapidly in the sun, and are unlikely to last for very long.

A far better option is reinforced plastic, which is much stronger physically and has much greater resistance to ultra-violet light. But best of all is fibreglass, which has none of the drawbacks of plastic and should last a lifetime if it is properly looked after.

Again, choose black or a dark colour to ensure that the pond looks reasonably natural, and make sure that there is an adequate shelf for marginal plants.

While this trough may not be attractive in itself, the addition of a pump and a water-spout creates a beautiful water feature.

Even a small trough of water will attract birds to the garden, but you may need to place a stone in it so that they can reach the water easily.

Concrete ponds

In many respects, concrete is still the best material. For large formal ponds it is the only choice, though the job of constructing them is best left to the experts; however, it is perfectly feasible to make your own smaller pond if you have some experience of concreting.

Use a hole whose sides slope at about 45°, 15cm (6in) larger than the final size of the pond, and line it with heavy polythene sheeting. Try to do the whole job in a single day, in order to reduce the possibility of leaks forming.

Cover the inside of the pond with a 10cm (4in) layer of concrete, and then cover this with reinforcing wire netting. If you want coloured concrete, now is the time to add the pigment to the mix. Give the

Hard edging of this kind would not be suited to an informal pond, but here its clean lines show that concrete can be an attractive medium. A narrow bed of *Acaena buchananii* has been placed around part of the pond.

pond a 5cm (2in) final layer of concrete, and trowel it smooth. Keep the concrete covered with wet hessian or a similar material so that it does not dry out too quickly and crack, and leave it for about 5 days, keeping the hessian damp.

Finally, treat the whole of the surface with a sealant such as Silglaze to prevent the lime in the concrete from harming the plants and fish.

Swimming-pools

If you have ever lived in a hot climate, you will know how important a swimming-pool can be. In northern Europe, swimming-pools have been a relative rarity until recently; people were put off by the cost, the need for regular maintenance, and of course the limited space they had available.

Mainly as a result of the fact that so many of us spend holidays in sunnier climes, and partly because of the increased interest in fitness, this attitude has changed. Swimming-pools are no longer regarded as the preserve of the super-rich, though they are still not cheap.

Things to think about when installing a pool

I have installed a number of swimming-pools in existing gardens, and these have usually proved a great success, provided the owners had a clear idea of what they could afford and had budgeted carefully

Here, a combination of spiky, rounded and feathery leaf forms has been used to great effect.

before they started. To keep costs down, you could leave out all the frills such as changing-rooms, showers, and diving-boards, and concentrate instead on the essentials.

Swimming-pools are usually lined with concrete or brick, which is then covered in a special thick liner, most commonly blue or green for that Mediterranean effect, but you can also choose black for a more natural, pond-like look.

It is important to have a proper cover, as this will ensure that the water stays clean, and will keep it warmer for a longer period of the year, as well as reduce the risk to small children. One possibility is simply to use nylon sheeting which floats on the surface of the water, but this is not very effective, as dirt and dead leaves can get through the gaps round the sides.

A better option is a cover made up of slats which rolls up and is stored in a water-filled container at the end of the pool. This has an inspection cover level with the side of the pool which can be lifted for cleaning. These covers are completely tight around the edges to keep out dirt, and can be opened and closed electrically.

Bog plants create a smooth transition from the pond to the rest of the garden, and provide an opportunity to grow plants which would not survive elsewhere.

Ponds for swimming in

I used decking to conceal the liner of this formal pond and to
create a link between the bridge and the pond.

The idea of a swimming-pond has still not caught on,
and many people will turn their noses up at the
suggestion of swimming in what they regard as dirty
water. But pond water does not have to be dirty; you
have complete control over it, which is often not the
case when you swim in a natural pond or river.

If you frequently use your pond for swimming, I
recommend that you change one third of the water
every 6 weeks. If it has its own biological or mechanical filtration system, this is not necessary.

The minimum size needed for swimming is about
10m^2 (110sq ft), though even this is only just big
enough for splashing around. To swim properly, you
will need a depth of between 80cm and 1.5m (32in

From a distance, the house seems almost to be smothered in plants, in this case gunnera and *Azalea* 'Harvest Moon'.

The same pond as that on the previous page; the round forms of hostas and *Hydrangea arborescens* contrast with the straight lines of the pond.

and 5ft), with a minimum length of 6m (20ft) so that you can swim a few strokes. Obviously, if you can afford something bigger, so much the better.

If you swim in a fairly small pond, this will seriously disturb the fish and other animals, so they will have to be placed elsewhere. In a large pond, you might have part of the pond sectioned off for swimming. One way of doing this is to build up the bottom of the pond so that it forms a wall starting about 15–25cm (6–10in) below the surface of the water, perhaps using heaped-up rocks. Do not build it any higher, as this will create a separation between the two parts of the pond and destroy the natural ecological balance which keeps the water clean. Alternatively, you may have to use a pump.

There is no reason why the planting should be kept to one part of the pond; if you place plants all around the edge, you will give it a more natural look and also help to prevent wave damage to the sides of the pond caused by people swimming.

A good size for a swimming-pond is about 40m² (430sq ft), of which about 10m² (110sq ft) is reserved for planting and the shallow area round the edges. A pond this size will also ensure that there is plenty of

room both for swimmers and fish and other animals. If the banks slope gently, use the middle of the pond as a swimming area, and use the whole bank of the pond for planting.

One way of filtering the pond is to have a separate, higher area where water flows first through a bed of aquatic plants which help to purify it, and then through a layer of gravel and sand to remove fine particles. The water then tumbles down into the swimming-pond in the form of a waterfall, which also helps to oxygenate the pond itself.

The part where you enter the water needs to be around 50cm (20in) deep, with a steeply sloping or vertical bank. If this is not possible, consider building a small jetty out into the deeper part of the water, with steps leading down into it.

Do not let people covered in suntan oil swim in the pond, for obvious reasons, and make sure that any electrical cables to the pump are kept well out of harm's way.

Pool covers with solar cells

Using a normal automatic pool cover of the kind described above will enable you to swim for 2–3 months longer than would otherwise be possible, as the cover helps the water to retain its warmth. If you want to maximize the time during which you can use the pool, it is possible to obtain covers with solar panels built into the slats. These are not cheap, but are certainly worth the investment.

One problem with most pool covers is the fact that they tend to be light in colour; it is a pity that they are not more readily available in various shades of green, so that they would blend in with the garden colours more easily.

Making a pool an integral part of the garden

One garden which I designed included a swimming-pool garden surrounded with yew hedges, which were also used elsewhere in the garden so that the pool formed a compartment of a larger whole. The owner did not want a bare area around the pool, and so I incorporated various features which made it into a garden in its own right. These included the deciduous *Gleditsia triacanthos* 'Inermis' or honey

The pond forms the gleaming centrepiece of this superb garden of roses, perennials, and topiary by the great designer Jacques Wirtz.

The rose bush has been used to create a screen, so that the raised formal pond comes as a surprise when you reach the end of the path.

locust, which has very delicate, fern-like leaves. The terrace was dotted with simple dark green rattan furniture and a variety of other plants such as maple and *Malus* 'Golden Hornet', with its small yellow crab-apples. On the second terrace, I placed a pergola covered in climbers and a simple green table and chairs.

More recently, I planted topiary box hedges around the edges of the pool, providing a lively evergreen backdrop which makes the pool look attractive even in winter. One important feature of this design was the fact that the pool was left uncovered and full of water in winter, when it was a cool, natural-looking greyish-blue. In summer, the pool is kept clean by an automatic vacuum cleaner. All the other pool equipment is kept in a flat-roofed wooden shed behind the hedge, as far as possible away from the patio, so that the gentle hum of the purifier plant is not audible.

Reducing the pool's visual impact

Another garden which I designed incorporated a pool in a fairly large garden. Here, I placed a low evergreen hedge between the house and the pool which screened one from the other. This meant that the owners did not have to look at the unattractive pool cover when the pool was not being used.

The cover also contained solar panels, with the result that the pool could be used as early as April without being artificially heated.

A luxurious heated swimming-pool in southern Belgium

I once designed a garden for a company headquarters, with a beautiful undulating area of grass surrounding a huge swimming-pool which had already been built by a colleague of mine.

Part of the pool was indoors, and part outside. The indoor part was in a glass pavilion, with the glass reaching down to the ground. The outside and inside parts were joined together; all you had to do was press a button, and the wall and glass screen would rise so that the two pools became one.

Because a glass screen had been used, there was no visual barrier between the two pools, and part of it could be used all year round. Unfortunately, not everyone can afford the luxury of a combined indoor and outdoor pool.

Twenty years ago, books and magazines were full of articles about particular swimming-pools in America, where the attitude towards what you can and cannot do has always been more flexible. In America, people let their imaginations run riot when it came to swimming-pools; partly under the influence of the Hollywood film industry, they spent fortunes creating dream palaces where nothing was too luxurious or eccentric, and flaunting their wealth to the cinema-going public. It was *de rigueur* for film stars such as Doris Day and Ava Gardner to have glamour photographs taken of them beside their swimming-pools, dining, chatting, swimming, or sipping dry martinis.

The swimming-pool played a crucial part in American culture, and elsewhere in the world it became synonymous with the easy-going American lifestyle. People began to imitate these pools, with their balustrades, elegant flights of steps, pool houses and luxurious garden furniture, when they saw them on their cinema and TV screens.

American-style decking combined with swimming-pools

When people want to build at low cost, they use local materials. In northern Europe, they use brick; in the United States, the most commonly available material is wood, which is why so many American houses since the time of the first pioneers have been made of timber. Later on there was a move towards building stone houses, but after the 1940s and 1950s the trend was reversed and people gradually turned back to using wood.

The timber used consisted mainly of hardwoods, and more specifically of redwood. This weathers attractively if it is not painted or treated, and is almost indestructible. Its colour harmonizes with

It would be difficult to achieve a greater contrast than here: the massive, jungle-like leaves of gunnera and the delicate foliage of bamboo rustling in the wind.

that of pine, beech and oak trees, which often have grey lichens growing on their trunks.

Many of the building techniques which the early settlers brought with them from Europe were not suited to the rugged terrain, where materials such as stone and brick were not always easily and cheaply available.

One of the solutions they found was to use wooden decking for those parts of their backyards which they used for relaxation. Decking is one of the most distinctive features of American gardens, and I have been using this versatile medium for decades in my own designs.

The neat, straight lines of decking also make it a good edging for ponds and swimming-pools, as it provides a point of transition between the man-made and natural components of the garden. Rocks can be brought in if they are not there already, mature trees are sometimes left standing, and the pool can be surrounded by arbours, pergolas, barbecues, and wooden screens. In the hot North American summers, the garden is treated simply as another room of the house, and the sense of continuity between the house and garden is reinforced by the fact that both use the same materials.

This raised oval pond looks circular when viewed from a distance, but more of the surface is visible than would be the case with a circular pond.

Despite the differences in climate, decking is starting to catch on in northern Europe. It used to be impractical because of this region's wet weather, but new ways of treating wood have meant that it is increasingly being used outdoors.

Round swimming-pools

The circle is a simple, pure form, which is why I mainly use it for large, imposing old buildings. There are few circular forms in nature – ovals are more common – and so a round swimming-pool can often look out of place in a garden. Keeping it clean can also be a problem, unless you can find a round cover to fit.

A round pool can look more attractive in winter if it is left uncovered and has its sides painted black, perhaps even using a statue or ornamental fountain to give it a more pond-like appearance. The other problem with round pools in this fitness-conscious age is that they cannot be used for swimming lengths.

A round swimming-pool in Bahia, Brazil

Brazil was conquered by the Portuguese, but it was also occupied by the Dutch for a time. In northern Brazil, there are many relics of this period in the form of sixteenth- and seventeenth-century buildings constructed at the instigation of the Dutch governor, Prince Maurits of Nassau. Plantations were created, many using slave labour, and large numbers of protestant churches were built. Few of these remain in modern-day Brazil, where most people are catholics or practise traditional religions.

The beautiful but poverty-stricken city of Bahia has countless historic monuments, including magnificent cathedrals, churches and shrines. Monks and nuns played an important role in the life of the city, providing medical care, education, and other services, and there were many monasteries and convents.

One convent has now been turned into a hotel, and I once stayed there with a group of garden-lovers I was taking on a tour of the country's gardens, including those of that world-famous Brazilian garden designer Roberto Burle Marx.

When we stayed in the convent, we were able to swim in the round pond which had once been its main source of water. Surrounded by chairs, potted palms and geraniums, the atmosphere was magical; it

This pond is located at some distance from the house, so that discovering it comes as a surprise.

Marx's own swimming-pool

Marx designed a truly spectacular garden for his own house, which again was a long, Portuguese-style building. He included a big pond-style swimming-pool with massive stone surrounds, where he would paint (he was also an artist) or entertain his many foreign guests.

The swimming-pool is supplied with fresh water from a fountain in a sculptural stone wall made of long interlocking slabs of stone. These come from the old city of Rio de Janeiro, large parts of which were being demolished to make way for new development at the time.

This pool is very clearly the work of a great artist. The wall is also planted with large-leafed climbing plants, and in front of it are some plants with upright foliage such as *Strelitzia* and the tree-fern, *Dicksonia antarctica*. An assortment of bromeliads have also been planted in the gaps in the wall.

still had something of the aura of bygone days, though it was now an earthly rather than a spiritual paradise. This was one example of a round swimming-pool which worked well, mainly because it was so large that you could swim lengths in it. The pool was also lit at night, giving it an added touch of glamour.

Turning a river into a swimming-pool

Roberto Burle Marx built many great gardens for offices and homes in Brazil. Some of these are located in and around the capital, Brasilia, and others elsewhere in the country. One is on a hillside near Rio, beside a long, typically Portuguese house with covered terraces on its shaded side. The terraces overlook a river, planted with large climbing plants such as *Monstera*, the Swiss cheese plant. Orchids grow in the trees, and the huge leaves of *Gunnera amazonica* hang over the river bank. The clear, cool water comes straight from the mountains; the owners did not need to build a swimming-pool, because the river provided a beautiful natural pool. They simply made the river wider and deeper, and then poured sand on to the riverbed. Here is a classic case where nature is far more beautiful than anything humans can build.

The zig-zag effect makes the pond appear to be part of a larger whole, perhaps a river.

A Japanese swimming-pool by the sea

On the large island of Shodoshima (*shima* means island) off the port of Kobe, there is a beautiful hotel overlooking Japan's inland sea. The whole island is a paradise for nature-lovers, with orchids, azaleas, camellias, magnolias, and hortensias all growing in the wild. Temples, perched high on the mountain-sides, rub shoulders with the modern Japanese- and European-style hotels. I have stayed in one of these hotels several times while visiting gardens and temples in the region. Sometimes alone, sometimes with fellow-travellers, I have walked from the hotel to the sea, which flows between two small islands. At low tide, it is possible to walk from the shore to the more distant of the two, but you have to be back again by high tide to avoid being swept away. The islands are covered in misshapen pine trees and

A big garden does not necessarily need a big pond to match.

rocky outcrops, and it takes a lot of good taste to design a swimming-pool amid so much natural beauty. The result is a long rectangle surrounded by grass and by the simple round forms of evergreen box-leafed or Japanese holly, *Ilex crenata*.

The pool has a low white concrete wall around it, on which you can sit and enjoy the view of the sea. The pool is a superb abstract composition, with the grey sea forming a powerful backdrop.

Ventimiglia: another hotel pool

Anyone who has travelled will have their own memories of their favourite swimming-pool. I was once on my way to Villa Hanbury, the Mediterranean garden in Italy, and stopped for a meal on the road near the French border. The hotel beside this busy road concealed a wonderful secret: a large courtyard with a brilliant blue swimming-pool. This was surrounded by seats and tables where people could sit in large groups.

Sometimes the best ponds and swimming-pools are where you least expect to find them.

Cape Town: a romantic formal swimming-pool

Many of the Dutch families who emigrated to South Africa built white houses in the style of their home country. A large number of these have survived, some of them transformed into hotels, restaurants and wineries.

The Alpihotel in Constantia, a suburb of Cape Town, is an imposing building with many outbuildings. These are former slaves' houses, which have now been converted into luxurious rooms for guests.

The stately interior has beautiful wooden floors, doors, and furniture, with wooden screens in the great hall. There are family portraits hanging on the walls, and big bouquets of flowers everywhere.

A long flight of steps with low white walls on either side decorated with lead sculptures leads out into the garden from the hotel. At the end of these steps is a simply designed swimming-pool. If you are sitting with the steps and the front of the hotel on one side of you, a wall on your other side separates the pool from the river which flows behind it.

In front of this wall, and directly outside the front door, stands a sculpture of a girl. She, along with the other parts of this architectural composition such as

the walls of the terrace and the front of the house, is painted white.

A few pots of flowering plants stand beside the girl, and the branches of some enormous oak trees hang over the wall behind her. There are large lawns on either side of the pool, and these are flanked in turn by more trees and gardens.

Southern France: a natural swimming-pool

I once designed the front patio for a beautiful house on a mountainside in southern France. A number of other garden designers had worked on other parts of the grounds.

There was a guest apartment beside the main house, and in front of it and to the left the land sloped gently downwards to an area planted with *Cistus*

This azure swimming-pool has been beautifully integrated within the overall fabric of a formal garden.

The view through the gaps in the hedge creates a sense of greater depth to the garden, and there is also an illusion in the foreground: the carpet of duckweed on the pond makes it look like an extension of the lawn behind.

One of the reasons why this dramatic water feature works is the fact that the colours of the materials are muted. Marble, concrete, or light-coloured materials would have created too much of a contrast with the surroundings.

and other Mediterranean plants. A simple sandy path wound its way through the cypress trees to a rocky outcrop which offered a magnificent view towards the Italian border.

The rock also served another purpose; it concealed the swimming-pool from the house and the guest apartment. The very natural-looking pool was blasted out of the rock using dynamite, and then filled with chlorinated water. The result was a superb pool, set amid rocks, native plants, and clusters of dark cypresses.

A swimming-pool converted into a pond

A colleague of mine, the garden designer Jacques Wirtz, designed an outdoor swimming-pool for a house in the East Flanders region of Belgium. This already had an indoor pool and a long pond in the garden, and the outdoor pool was placed between the two in order to create an almost continuous line of water. The outdoor pool had been painted blue, and the water in the pond behind it had a strong greenish tinge.

A few years later, the outdoor pool was itself converted into a pond, so that all the water outside the house was the same colour: green when the sun was not shining, and blue when it was.

The result is a very grand composition which is full of drama. It shows how hedges, steps, rectangular forms, and grass can go superbly together, and how blue-walled swimming-pools should not be placed beside natural water if the two are to form a single entity. It is better either to keep the two separate using a hedge, or to solve the problem by painting the outdoor pool black.

Right: The apotheosis of water gardening. Here, water is the dominant feature of the garden, with raised pools serving a similar function to flowerbeds.

This pond has been dramatically edged with large swathes of moisture-loving ferns on one side and *Primula pulverulenta* on the other.

Right: This house originally sat rather oddly on its plot of land; it seemed out of proportion, with the front garden twice as large as the back garden. I tried to redesign it so that the owners would be enticed out into the front garden, and this seems to have been a success. I placed a big formal pond widthwise opposite the house, with a lawn creating a sense of space and linking the two together. A grassy path leads between the borders from the drive to the lawn; further down the drive a bitumen path leads to the front door through borders of pink, blue, and purple flowers with rows of acacias behind them. The pond has a tall yew hedge around three sides, behind which is an elegant bench and more herbaceous borders. Beyond the hedge, tall trees and bamboos give added privacy, so that the front garden is now a haven of seclusion from the outside world.

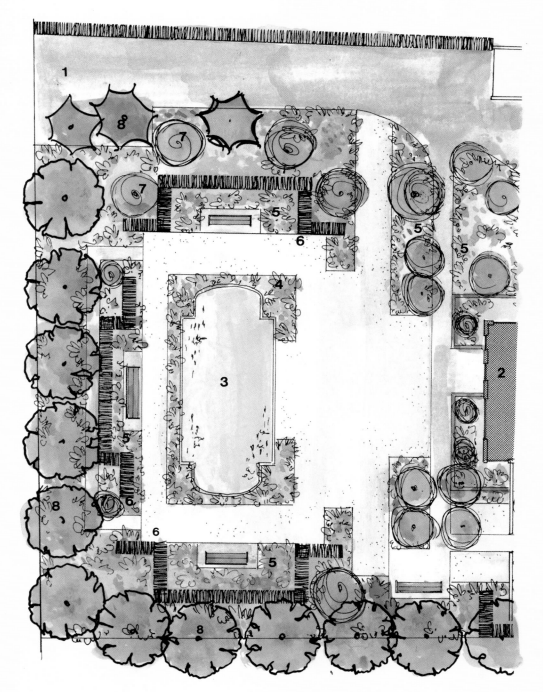

1   drive

2   house

3   pond using PVC liner and wooden edging

4   low-growing plants: ivy, hosta, and pink *Rosa* 'The
    Fairy'

5   tall perennials such as *Anemone vitifolia*, *Lythrum
    virgatum* 'Rose Queen', *Miscanthus sinensis*
    'Gracillimus', and roses

6   yew hedges

7   tall evergreen bamboo

8   existing dense wall of pines, cherry laurels, and holly

CHAPTER 8

The choice of flower and leaf colour

Using colours beside the water

There are many plants with yellow flowers which look as though they are most at home beside the water. One good example is *Ligularia*, of which there are several species with large rounded leaves similar to those of the invasive ground-covering perennial, *Petasites hybridus*. In dry conditions, its large leaves become limp when the sun shines on them, but return to normal afterwards.

Ligularia dentata 'Othello' is a variety with butter-yellow daisy-like flowers, which reaches a height of around 1.5m (5ft). *L. dentata* 'Desdemona' has purple leaves and orange flowers which do not always go well with those of other plants. The yellow of *L. dentata* 'Othello' makes it an ideal companion for the similarly coloured flowers of *L. punctata*, or the soft yellow of *Kirengeshoma palmata*. The latter has funnel-shaped flowers which hang downwards and contrast with the upright stems of *Ligularia* and *Lysimachia*. All of these harmonize particularly well with the spreading ornamental grass, *Spartina pectinata* 'Aureo Marginata', also known as *S. pectinata* 'Aureo-variegata'. This has strong, upright stems and arching leaves which sway in the wind, contrasting starkly with the prominent rounded leaves of the *Ligularia*.

Woodland plants and a tall *Metasequoia glyptostroboides* growing in the gardens of Walenburg Castle in the Netherlands.

What goes with orange flowers such as Ligularia dentata 'Desdemona'?

I tend to be cautious about using orange in the garden, which of course is unjustified. A group of orange plants can be very effective at creating a vivid splash of colour, provided there is plenty of green around to neutralize it. It is even possible to design a whole border of orange plants, which creates a distinctively cheerful effect.

Alstroemeria auriantiaca 'Orange King' is a brilliantly coloured plant which in the right conditions produces large numbers of flowers in a lively shade of orange with streaks of yellow and red. Try planting this with the orange flowers of *Trollius* 'Goldquelle' or 'Orange Princess', or with the orange and yellow flowers of the red-hot poker, *Kniphofia*. The leaf shapes of these three plants also provide some interesting contrasts: *Ligularia* has round leaves; those of *Trollius* are also round, but incised; and *Alstroemeria* has narrow, twisted leaves. *Kniphofia*, on the other hand, has long narrow leaves which grow upwards and bend under their own weight.

Neat bands of colour are provided by (from top to bottom) the enormous leaves of gunnera, astilbe, and the sulphur-yellow flowers of *Primula florindae*, better known as the giant cowslip.

A combination of blue moisture-loving plants

One plant which suits just about any position but has a slight preference for moist soil is *Iris sibirica*. It reaches a height of about 1m (3ft), and has long, very narrow bright green leaves. Because of its similarity to the yellow flag, *Iris pseudacorus*, people tend to think that *Iris sibirica* also needs boggy conditions. There is also a white garden variety, *Iris sibirica* 'Alba'.

The long leaves of irises need to be placed beside something contrasting or they will soon start to look untidy after the plant has flowered. One suitable candidate is *Brunnera macrophylla*, which will grow anywhere but is particularly suited to positions in semi-shade and beside streams. It has beautiful blue flowers like those of the forget-me-not which appear in early spring, and round green leaves.

Equally attractive are the bright blue flower spikes of *Veronica* 'Shirley Blue', though this becomes a rather dull and shapeless clump of greenery after it has flowered.

One very easy plant to grow is *Campanula portenschlagiana*, a vigorous, prostrate perennial with fairly long, thin stems and blue, bell-shaped flowers. This will flower again if the stems are cut back.

Finally, for tall blue accent plants, use delphiniums or *Veronica virginiana*. Neither of these looks particularly like a pondside plant, but they have a very distinctive vertical habit.

Wild plants as inspiration for a damp garden

Why is it that plants growing wild by a ditch, bog or stream are often so much more inspiring than an artificially planted pondside? I think this is partly due to the enormous variety of plants growing side by side, such as the long, green stems of grasses and the compact forms of yellow flag, valerian, geum, or purple loosestrife.

Nature also manages to mix colours with an effortless skill and boldness of combinations far surpassing that of any artist. It is therefore important to learn from plants growing in the wild, seeing how, for example, yellow water buttercups somehow harmonize with light pink valerian and the greyish pink of liverwort. The main reason why this works is because there is so much green foliage to tone down the bright colours. Many gardeners seem intent on cramming as much colour and as little foliage as possible into their gardens; this is a mistake, as the subtlety of nature shows.

Sometimes, colour combinations in the wild are so striking that it is difficult not to believe there is some kind of guiding hand behind them. How is it, for example, that we can find three white-flowered plants, such as *Lysimachia*, *Achillea ptarmica*, and *Achillea millefolium*, all growing side by side in the wild?

At other times, too, I have seen extraordinary combinations of purple and pink growing beside streams that make me want to go back home and grab my camera.

Gunnera is for those with plenty of space to spare;
Peltiphyllum peltatum **is a much more compact alternative,**
and a splash of yellow is provided by marsh marigolds.

I have seen reddish-purple hemp agrimony, *Eupatorium cannabinum*, jostling for space with pale pink *Stachys palustris* and the occasional purple-flowered *Symphytum*.

I have also seen combinations of yellow wild flowers which have stopped me in my tracks, such as the creeping Jenny, *Lysimachia nummularia*, growing beside the water together with its taller relative, *Lysimachia vulgaris* or common loosestrife. There are countless combinations of yellow-flowering plants, from the ordinary buttercup to the large water buttercup, which prefers to have damp soil around its roots.

There are also many blue wild flowers which also look good side by side, from campanula to gentian and the skullcap, *Scutellaria galericulata*, which grows in water meadows with rich soils. But purple, white, and yellow are the colours which dominate the water's edge and the water itself.

In nature, there is never a clear dividing line between wet and dry soils. There are plenty of plants which will grow in the mud beside a pond at this point of transition between the two environments. One example is another blue plant, the water forget-me-not *Myosotis palustris*, which weaves itself delicately between the more large-leafed marginal plants; another is the water mint, *Mentha aquatica*, which will spread to cover the edges of a pond.

However, this group of moisture-lovers includes relatively few plants with blue flowers; there is a much greater selection of pink and yellow ones. The flowering rush, *Butomus umbellatus*, is popular mainly for its umbels of pink flowers; its long, narrow leaves are much less eye-catching.

Alisma plantago-aquatica, otherwise known as the water plantain, has pale pink, almost white flowers on long, upright stalks and bright green oval leaves. Each segment of the flower stalk has three more or less horizontal lateral stems with conical panicles of flowers in summer. These are the main aquatics with pink flowers, but there are many bog plants of this colour. The best-known is *Iris pseudacorus*, which has bright yellow flowers followed by large clusters of green fruits. These burst open in the autumn to reveal highly decorative orange seeds.

The butter-yellow *Ranunculus lingua* 'Grandiflora' is a tall ornamental plant which grows among other aquatic plants such as irises, water plantain, and reeds. It has large, saucer-shaped flowers and is suited to most damp situations.

Another yellow-flowered native plant which you will see growing by the waterside is the moisture-loving member of the loosestrife family, *Lysimachia thyrsifolia*. Its compact growth habit and limited height of about 30cm (12in) mean that it is not a particularly impressive plant.

A more eye-catching specimen is *Inula britannica*, which reaches a height of about 1m (3ft) and has daisy-like orange or yellow flowers. This might be juxtaposed with its garden relative, *Inula hookeri*,

which has similar flowers but grows to a height of around 1.5m (5ft).

A very different yellow-flowering aquatic plant is the golden club, *Orontium aquaticum*. This is a very useful plant which makes a good foil for many others. It has attractive glossy foliage which stands upright above the surface of the water, and displays unusual white pencil-shaped flower heads with golden yellow tips.

There is one colour which we might easily forget in this overview of moisture-loving native plants, and that is white. This colour has just as many complex variations as pink and yellow, as you will see if you compare, for example, frogbit, watercress, and arrowhead. Frogbit grows very quickly and can cover large areas of water. Watercress, or *Nasturtium*

The spiky foliage gives this garden and its pond a quite unmistakably Mediterranean feel.

officinale, has very different requirements: it needs plenty of oxygen, and actually prefers moving water. If you want to grow watercress, which makes a wonderful salad vegetable, you will need a pond, barrel, or trough, and a pump to keep the water circulating. The plant reaches a maximum height of about 20cm (8in).

The arrowhead, *Sagittaria sagittifolia*, is a slightly taller plant, also with white flowers. These are larger and more easily recognizable, consisting of three white petals and a dark purple centre. The leaves,

Campanula lactiflora 'Loddon Anna' frames this dainty-looking bed of day lilies in a variety of colours, with conifers providing greenery in the winter.

The same pond as that on the left, almost invisible beneath a dense carpet of water lilies, contrasting with the long leaves of the daylilies.

too, are easy to identify; as the plant's name suggests, they resemble arrows.

Another less well known shallow-water marginal or bog plant is cotton grass, or *Eriophorum*. This grows in moorland areas and needs an acid soil and acid water, and has fluffy white seed heads in mid- to late summer. It should not be combined with fast-spreading plants because it can very quickly become swamped by them. Place it in a sunny position in a part of the pond where it can grow undisturbed. The species you are most likely to find on sale is *Eriophori angustifolium*, which grows to a height of about 45cm (18in).

If you combine plants with differently coloured flowers, always remember the lesson which nature teaches us: there is no reason why you should not do so, provided there is plenty of green foliage or stems to offset them.

Leaf shape and flower colour in aquatic plants

White and yellow are the two most common colours among flowering aquatic plants. One of the plants most often grown in ponds apart from water lilies is the brandy bottle, *Nuphar lutea*, which has large buttercup-like flowers and round leaves rather like those of the water lily. This spreads to cover a large area, and is not really suitable for small garden ponds unless you regularly ensure that it is kept in check; *Nuphar minima*, also known as *Nuphar pumila*, is a better choice in this situation. Water gentian is another yellow-flowered plant which can become a nuisance if allowed to spread; plants like these are best grown in large baskets or other containers which prevent the plants from becoming invasive and can easily be fished out of the water for maintenance. If you do grow them in the soil at the bottom of the pond, the roots can be pulled up quite easily using a rake.

Bladderwort, or *Utricularia*, is another yellow-flowered plant; its leaves float just below the surface, and the flowers extend about 10cm (4in) above the water. The bladderwort is a carnivorous plant; it has bladders on its leaves and stems which capture and digest microscopic animals. It prefers a shaded position.

There are also a large number of yellow-flowering water lilies in shades ranging from pale to bright yellow, but these are hybrids and therefore do not belong in this chapter.

Of the white aquatic plants, *Nymphaea alba* is native to the whole of northern Europe, but it has large round leaves which quickly take over in a small area of water; again, I always plant them in a container, and when the leaves start to cover too much of the surface I simply snip them off. Water lilies play an important part in shading the surface of the water, thereby reducing algae growth and keeping fish and other aquatic animals comfortable in summer. The leaves also give off oxygen, though this job is done more effectively by plants whose leaves grow below the surface of the water.

One of the few oxygenating plants which has decorative flowers is the water buttercup, *Ranunculus aquatilis*. Most of its foliage lies

All the plants behind the stone pond edging are drought-tolerant: maiden pinks, sea pinks, and primulas in a variety of shades.

The formal zigzag shape of this pond contrasts with the large groups of luxuriant plant growth. Again, gunnera dominates every other plant in the garden.

underwater, and the small white flowers consisting of five oval petals appear just above the surface. Although not invasive, it can be kept from spreading too far by placing it in a container of relatively poor, sandy soil.

Another of the few flowering oxygenators is the water violet, *Hottonia palustris*. This has spikes of white to pale lilac flowers which appear up to 15cm (6in) above the water in early summer, and evergreen feathery leaves which make ideal winter protection for fish and other animals. Its relative, *Hottonia inflata*, has white flowers.

This pond margin features dramatic contrasts between the lance-shaped leaves of irises and the rounded foliage of variegated hostas.

Right: The contrasting planting on either side of this rectangular pond provides a riot of colour.

On the left of the pond are two long mixed borders of herbaceous perennials, roses, and shrubs. The edge of the pond has been planted with *Hosta fortunei* 'Aureomarginata', *Alchemilla mollis*, and a host of other plants.

The other side of the pond has been laid to grass, which has been planted with wild flowers and is left unmown in summer. A huge variety of plants grow more or less randomly in this meadow, including large numbers of poppies and cornflowers.

At either end of the pond is a terrace, with the tiles jutting out over the water's edge to hide the pond liner, which is held down by railway sleepers or ties.

Many aquatic and bog plants have lance-shaped leaves: these cream and blue irises go particularly well with reedmace and yellow flag.

I hope this overview of native water plants is a source of inspiration, particularly if you prefer your pond to look as natural as possible. But whichever aquatic plants you choose, remember that their decorative value is of secondary importance: the right balance of plants is essential if the ecological balance of your pond is to be preserved.

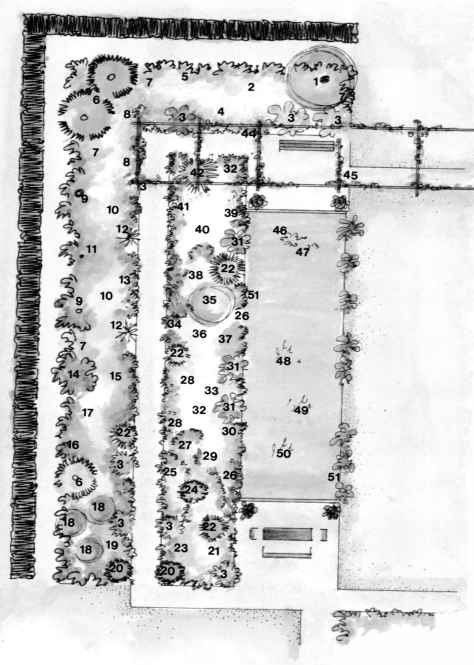

13 *Viburnum davidii*
14 *Spiraea arguta*
15 *Iberis* 'Snowflake'
16 *Stranvaesia davidiana*
17 *Stephanandra incisa* 'Crispa'
18 *Amelanchier lamarckii*
19 *Pachysandra terminalis*
20 *Chamaecyparis*
21 *Cimicifuga dahurica*
22 *Miscanthis sinensis*
    'Gracillimus'
23 *Helleborus niger*
24 *Juniperus*
25 *Anaphalis triplinervis*
26 *Alchemilla mollis*
27 *Rosa* 'Schneewittchen'
28 *Buphthalmum salicifolium*
29 *Ligularia przewalskii*
30 *Filipendula ulmaria*
31 *Hosta fortunei* 'Aureomarginata'
32 *Kirengeshoma palmata*
33 *Geranium sanguineum* 'Album'
34 *Campanula carpatica*
35 *Malus* 'Golden Hornet'
36 *Lysimachia punctata*
37 *Iris pseudacorus*
38 *Rosa* 'Allgold'
39 *Iris sibirica*
40 *Mollis azalea* 'Adriaan Koster'
41 *Rudbeckia speciosa*
42 *Sinarundinaria murielae*
43 *Rosa* 'Golden Showers'
44 *Lonicera periclymenum*
45 *Wisteria sinensis* 'Alba'
46 *Pontederia cordata*
47 *Sagittaria sagittifolia*
48 *Nymphaea marliacea* 'Albida'
49 *Nymphaea marliacea*
    'Chromatella'
50 *Typha angustifolia*
51 *Caltha palustris*

1 *Betula papyrifera*
2 *Rhododendron* 'Golden Flare'
3 *Hedera helix* 'Arborescens'
4 *Skimmia japonica* 'Foremanii'
5 *Rosa* 'Nevada'
6 *Pinus nigra austriaca*

7 *Lamium galeobdolon*
8 *Rhododendron* 'Madame Mason'
9 *Malus floribunda*
10 *Rhododendron* 'Persil'
11 *Aralia elata*
12 *Pennisetum compressum*

CHAPTER 9

The biggest leaves of them all: the gunnera

Plants which look as though they belong by the water

Large-leafed perennials need plenty of water; at least that is the impression given by plants such as *Hosta*, *Gunnera*, *Peltiphyllum*, and *Ligularia*. Those perennials with large leaves which prefer dry conditions, such as the cotton or Scotch thistle, *Onopordum*, are the exceptions which prove the rule.

Simply planting these in a garden can give it a rainforest-like feel; their extravagant growth habit suggests hot, wet, fertile conditions. They are at their best in summer, particularly after a sudden downpour of rain.

When designing a garden, it is worth allocating a specific section of it to these large-leafed perennials. You have a choice between those which do not actually need humid conditions, but look as though they do, and those which will grow equally happy in dry or moist conditions.

The gunnera is a common plant in the vast rainforests and marshlands of Brazil's Amazon river, but can also be grown in temperate climates.

Petasites hybridus **has leaves similar to those of the gunnera,
but considerably smaller. It bears white or pink flowers in
late winter.**

Plants which do not require moist soil

One of the cardinal rules in designing a garden is to
group plants together to create compositions, rather
than simply buying the individual species and
varieties which appeal to you and sticking them in
the ground.

For example, you might want a group of tall plants to
screen part of the garden from view, or to create
privacy from the neighbours. One such grouping
which does not need particularly damp soil might
start with *Macleaya cordata*, which can sometimes
reach a height of 2m (6ft 6in) and has bluish-grey,
lobed leaves; this is known as the plume poppy
because of its feathery panicles of beige-coloured
flowers. The long, wide green leaves of *Polygonum
amplexicaule* go well with those of the *Macleaya*;
this is a moisture-loving plant which will also
tolerate normal garden soil provided it is not too dry.

It bears large spikes of bright red flowers over a
period of several months in the summer and autumn.
There is also a beautiful pink variety of this *Polygonum*: *P. amplexicaule* 'Roseum'. This reaches a
similar height of about 1.2m (4ft).

These tall plants could be surrounded by low-
growing ones such as astilbe, which comes in many
different shades of pink.

Another plant which harmonizes well with *Macleaya* is *Centranthus ruber* or red valerian, with its
small, star-shaped pink or white flowers. This needs
reasonably well-drained soil, but will grow in poor
soils and exposed locations where other plants
would struggle to survive.

Growing large-leafed plants beside a pond

Other plants with large leaves tend to need moist
conditions because more water evaporates from their
leaves, particularly in warm weather. This is why so
many of them prefer shade or semi-shade. If you do
want to plant them in full sun, they will need a
proper water supply if they are to have a chance of

**Like any other plant, gunnera gains considerably from being
juxtaposed with different plants, in this case *Bergenia* and
Matteucia.**

surviving. You can provide this by creating a marshy area of soil using plastic sheeting to prevent the water from draining away.

The other alternative is to use some kind of sprinkler or irrigation system. If you only get round to spraying the plants when you remember to do so, or when the soil appears to have dried out, there is a risk of underwatering. A better method is to use meters so that the plants are automatically watered as soon as the soil moisture falls below a certain level.

Walda Pairon's gunneras

The famous garden designer Walda Pairon has a large group of *Gunnera amazonica* growing behind her house. As its name suggests, this species grows in the marshes alongside Brazil's biggest river. It has short stems and huge puckered leaves, 1.5–2m (5ft–6ft 6in) across, with pronounced ribs and a hand-shaped structure of veins. It bears fruit during the summer, though these are not fertile in a northern European climate.

If this plant is looked after properly, it is easily the most spectacular of all foliage plants for a damp garden. Its roots must be kept moist, but not soaking wet, so do not plant it directly in a pond or a bog garden. It can be watered using a hose hidden between the plants, perhaps with a drip system. Walda Pairon's gunneras are planted about 10m (30ft) from the house, separated from it by a terrace with a beautiful Lutyens bench and an old, rough-hewn wooden table in the middle. She frequently places sculptures or other attractive objects on the table to make the view from the window more dramatic, and the huge leaves of the gunnera render it even more so.

Growing gunnera in pots

The Belgian garden of St-Truiden, near Antwerp, is located far enough inland to give it much colder winters than places nearer the moderating influence of the sea. It still manages to grow gunneras by keeping them in pots, and this has the added advantage that the plants can be moved around at will. A number of them have therefore been used as accent plants on a large, covered terrace. I had not realized until I visited this garden that gunneras did not require constant moisture: dishes were placed

Gaudi, the Spanish Art Nouveau architect, made hedges from palms. Here, the garden designer Anthony Paul has created one using *Petasites hybridus*.

underneath the pots and filled from time to time so the soil was moist, but not soaking wet.

Using gunneras as accent plants

I once did some work on a tiny urban garden only 5 x 5m (16 x 16ft). The owners wanted a garden which was purely for looking at, and had no interest in sitting or walking around in it. I therefore built a circular pond 3m (10ft) in diameter in the middle of the garden, and placed a single gunnera behind it, completely dominating the garden.

The brilliant red plumes of *Astilbe* 'Spinel' make a wonderful contrast with the large leaves of *Peltiphyllum peltatum*.

This delicate, moisture-loving herbaceous plant is *Chaerophyllum hirsutum* 'Roseum'.

I also placed a few low-growing plants around the pond, consisting of ferns, lady's mantle (*Alchemilla mollis*), and ivy, along with two ornamental evergreen bamboos. The only other plant was a water lily in the pond. The result was an almost completely maintenance-free garden, and yet it was full of drama, particularly when the leaves of the gunnera began to open.

Another garden I once discovered in the Dutch town of Heerlen was surrounded by a white wall. I stepped out of the living-room into a tranquil little oasis of total privacy, with a large, pastel-coloured canvas parasol adding to the sunny Mediterranean feeling. The garden contained a single accent plant in the form of a young but flourishing gunnera. This was surrounded by the ground-cover plant *Acaena buchananii* which, in complete contrast to the gunnera, tolerates hot, dry conditions. This might seem a rather strange combination on paper, but it worked very well.

The gunneras by the moat at Walenburg Castle

Not all of us are fortunate enough to have a moat outside our homes, but that of Walenburg Castle in the Netherlands provides an ideal environment for a

large, healthy specimen of gunnera. In winter, it is wrapped in a thick layer of beech leaves to protect it against frost. These are held in place by positioning chicken-wire about 60cm (24in) high round the plant, and then pouring them into the top. The bigger the circle of chicken-wire, the less likely the plant is to be affected by frost. In summer, the leaves appear about 1m (3ft) above the water level in the moat, just one of the many dramatic features of this castle and its beautiful gardens.

The famous gunnera at Stourhead

If you want to see just how big this plant can grow, have a look at the famous landscaped gardens of Stourhead in Wiltshire, England. In the eighteenth century, Henry Hoare began building what he called a "philosophical garden", using forms from Greek mythology to express philosophical ideas. One is the fountain, which symbolizes the source of all life; the garden also has lakes with paths round them representing man's path through life, and beside one lake are a temple and a mausoleum in the Graeco-Roman style which was so popular in Italy.

The temple is dedicated to love, and the mausoleum is a reminder of the inevitability of death. A bridge over the lake symbolizes eternity, and the fact that we are always moving forward into the unknown.

Beside the Roman-style stone bridge are the enormous leaves of a gunnera, 2–3m (6ft 6in–10ft) across, one of the most photographed plants in garden literature. This is a more recent addition; Henry Hoare would not have dreamed of using such an exotic plant. Early landscape architects were interested only in native English trees, shrubs, and aquatic plants, as these helped to blur the boundary between the garden and the surrounding woods and farmland.

The gunnera at Wörlitz

One of the most interesting large gardens in eastern Germany is Wörlitz, beside the river Elbe. This area is the German equivalent of the Brenta Canal in Italy, with its magnificent Palladian villas. Kings, princes, counts, and barons built their pleasure-gardens along the Elbe, but Wörlitz is unique among

This unusual, spiky plant is *Heracleum giganticum*; it has considerable decorative value even in winter.

this series of riverside residences and gardens in that the river has actually been diverted through it, to create lakes and sinuous water features. The garden is traversed by boat, and it was here that I saw gunneras being protected against frosts using polystyrene foam.

A wooden box with a removable lid was placed over the plants, and filled with the foam. This has a number of advantages: it is a lightweight material, with good insulation properties, but its drawback is the fact that it looks so unattractive.

I was also interested to find that these plants indigenous to a hot country could clearly survive the rigours of winter in a continental climate like Germany's.

These converging rows of water lilies and perennials lead the eye towards the gunnera and the neatly pruned *Pyrus salicifolia* in the distance.

**The leaves of the ornamental rhubarb, *Rheum tanguticum*,
are similar in shape to those of the gunnera, as are the
leaves of Rodgersia.**

Protecting gunnera from spring frosts

One of the most difficult times of year for this plant
is the spring. In a warm spring, the new shoots will
start growing through the protecting layer, and it will
need to be removed immediately so that their growth
is not impeded. If not, the shoots will be pale, lanky,
and very susceptible to sun, wind, rain, and hail.

It is therefore important to keep an eye on the
weather forecast, and provide gunneras with proper
protection against frosty damage. The gunnera in the
garden of Walenburg Castle has large fishermen's
umbrellas placed over the leaves, which seems to
help. Jute sacks or plastic sheeting placed over the
leaves work just as well.

**Right: In a large garden such as this one, it is possible to
have a whole series of different environments. In the
average postage-stamp suburban garden, it is better to
concentrate on only one.**

**This example has a large double border, a vegetable and
cut-flower garden, a shade area, a herb garden, and a
water garden.**

**There is a temptation to put every plant under the sun
in a garden this size, but even here you cannot give your
imagination a completely free rein. A selection of large-
leafed plants – including a gunnera, of course – were
therefore placed around the lake, together with
hortensias, Lythrum, astilbe, and candelabra primulas.
Here, in the Belgian region of Brabant, the climate
means that the gunnera has to be covered in winter. As
it then becomes something of an eyesore, it has been
placed well away from the house.**

a	public road
b	path
c	oaks
d	pond and bog garden in copse
e	outhouses
f	car park and hedge
g	entrance to garage
h	house
i	perennials
j	terrace
k	ponds
l	pink and blue borders
m	herb garden
n	bridge leading to arbour in middle of lake
o	white hortensia garden
p	vegetable garden with pergola covered in fruit

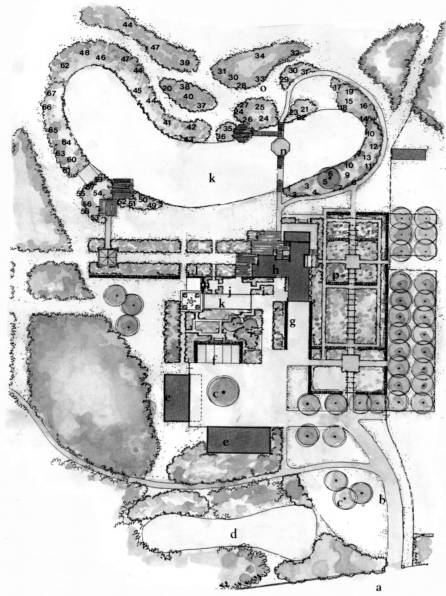

32 *Hypericum androsaemum*

33 *Hydrangea macrophylla* 'Mariesii Perfecta'

34 *Magnolia soulangiana*

35 *Rosa* 'Mozart'

36 *Hydrangea quercifolia*

37 *Pyrus salicifolia*

38 *Eleagnus angustifolia*

39 *Hydrangea paniculata*

40 *Rodgersia aesculifolia*

41 *Pennisetum compressum*

42 *Geranium endressii* 'Wargrave Pink'

43 *Gunnera manicata*

44 *Abies veitchii*

45 *Peltiphyllum peltatum*

46 *Miscanthus sin.* 'Gracillimus'

47 *Rhododendron* 'Pink Pearl'

48 *Hydrangea aspera*

49 *Rosa multiflora*

50 *Hosta sieb.* 'Elegans' (*H. glauca* 'Robusta')

51 *Rosa* 'White Fleurette'

52 *Teucrium chamaedrys*

53 *Taxus baccata* – bollen

54 *Anemone* 'Honorine Jobert'

55 *Hydrangea macrophylla* 'Mariesii Perfecta'

56 *Cimicifuga racemosa*

57 *Hosta fortunei* 'Aureomarginata'

58 *Lythrum* 'Morden's Pink'

59 *Gunnera*

60 *Pinus cembra*

61 *Hydrangea quercifolia*

62 *Hosta crispula*

63 *Prunus yedoensis*

64 *Hydrangea serrata* 'Blue Bird'

65 *Hydrangea paniculata*

66 *Magnolia soulangiana*

67 *Prunus laurocerasus* 'Zabeliana'

1 *Gunnera manicata*

2 *Lythrum* 'Morden's Pink'

3 *Peltiphyllum peltatum*

4 *Geranium endressii* 'Wargrave Pink'

5 *Rosa* 'Mozart'

6 *Miscanthus sin.* 'Gracillimus'

7 *Pennisetum compressum*

8 *Euphorbia wulfenii*

9 *Osmunda regalis*

10 *Peltiphyllum peltatum*

11 *Hosta crispula*

12 *Kirengeshoma palmata*

13 *Hedera colchica*

14 *Ligularia przewalskii*

15 *Hydrangea arborescens*

16 *Miscanthus sin.* 'Silberfeder'

17 *Eupatorium purpureum*

18 *Miscanthus sin.* 'Gracillimus'

19 *Rosa* 'Smarty'

20 *Euphorbia wulfenii*

21 *Cornus controversa*

22 *Gunnera*

23 *Rosa* 'Nevada'

24 *Taxodium distichum*

25 *Hydrangea serrata* 'Blue Bird'

26 *Ilex aquifolium* 'J.C. van Tol'

27 *Malus sargentii*

28 *Tsuga heterophylla*

29 *Prunus laurocerasus* 'Zabeliana'

30 *Ligustrum quihoui*

31 *Hosta undulata*

CHAPTER 10

Hostas, petasites, lythrum, and other large-leafed plants

Large-leafed perennials with many different uses

If you are fed up with the constant battle to protect hostas against slugs and snails, you can use slug pellets and risk harming other wildlife in the garden, or you can stop trying to grow hostas at all. But if neither of these solutions is acceptable, try growing them in pots, where they will thrive with proper care and are less likely to end up with their leaves shredded. They also look very good if one kind of hosta is planted in each of a number of terracotta, lead or wooden containers.

Hostas come in a great variety of leaf sizes and colours, and you are bound to find something which suits your taste and the amount of space you have available. They are indigenous to Japan and China, and prefer semi-shade and a damp situation, but will not tolerate constantly wet conditions such as those of a bog garden. They will thrive in peat or clay soils, both of which retain moisture well, but sandy soils will need to be improved by adding peat.

A striking combination of the dull green foliage and yellow flowers of *Lysimachia punctata* with the blue leaves and very pale lilac flowers of *Hosta sieboldiana* 'Elegans'.

Hosta undulata **has large green leaves and white flowers, similar in colour to those of the *Rodgersia tabularis* to its right.**

Every gardener has his or her favourites, and the following are some of mine. The best-known is probably *Hosta sieboldiana* 'Elegans', which has bluish-grey leaves which can grow to a considerable size in the right conditions. Its flowers are nothing special, and it is grown mainly for its foliage.

Hosta undulata, on the other hand, has very attractive white flowers and bright green leaves, though if the plant is kept in the sun this colour will fade.

Hosta fortunei 'Aureomarginata' has green leaves with yellow edges, and violet flowers which again are not as attractive as the leaves. This variety looks best when planted in groups.

Hosta crispula resembles the previous variety, but has white rather than yellow edges. All hostas have leaves whose veins originate from a single point at the end of the leaf-stalk, and in *Hosta crispula* these are very prominent, which gives the plant added decorative value.

Hosta sieboldiana 'Francis Williams' has large blue leaves and greenish-yellow edges; this unlikely combination of colours actually works quite well. If you place it against a plain background, the leaves can look spectacular. I once saw a walled courtyard garden lined with many terracotta pots of this plant and with old, slightly fading rattan chairs; the result was very picturesque.

I grow *Hosta fortunei* 'Albopicta' in pots, but I never manage to pluck up the courage to plant them in my clients' gardens because they have such bright yellow leaves. It is their colour which makes them look so good in containers, and they fade to dull green during the summer.

Hosta fortunei 'Hyacinthina' is one of the many small-leafed hostas. It has bluish-green foliage, and is particularly suited to smaller gardens, or to being grown in combination with large-leafed plants. It has glossy leaves which do not dominate the garden as much as those of its larger relatives. *Hosta lancifolia* has similarly small leaves to those of *Hosta fortunei*, but these are dark green and the flowers are purple.

Rodgersia aesculifolia **has creamy-white flowers and attractive crinkled leaves. In the foreground is a group of common female ferns.**

Petasites, an invasive large-leafed plant

Very few large-leafed plants spread as quickly as *Petasites*, which constantly seeks out new territory to conquer with its horizontal underground runners. It has daisy-like flowers on tall stalks. *Petasites hybridus* is more commonly grown in gardens, and has greenish-white flowers very early in the spring. I still remember a holiday in Germany where I stumbled on the purplish-pink variety growing in the melting snow beside a stream. I had never seen it before, and took some photographs, convinced I had made a major new discovery. But when I got home, I found that it commonly grew in such inhospitable places as roadside ditches and demolition sites. The

Hosta sieboldiana 'Frances Williams' offers a combination of leaf colours which is unusual in the plant world: blue and yellow. It is a beautiful plant, not least when its pale lilac, almost white flowers appear. On the left is *Peltiphyllum*.

best way of growing this plant is to restrict its root growth by planting it in a buried plastic bucket with some drainage holes bored into it.

I have been growing petasites in a trough by the front door of my canalside house for years. It flourishes provided that I water it regularly and keep it out of the sun; otherwise, it very quickly wilts.

Peltiphyllum peltatum is another invasive plant, and has clusters of pink and white flowers which appear in spring, before the leaves.

Rheum palmatum-tanguticum is the ornamental

Plants with bright colours or large leaves in the distance help to foreshorten a large garden. Here, that plant is the blue-leafed *Hosta sieboldiana* 'Elegans'.

Two very different variegated plants with white edges: on the left of the sundial is *Hosta undulata* 'Crispula', and on the right is the grass *Phalaris arundinacea* 'Picta'.

relative of *Rheum*, the common rhubarb. It has pink flowers and bluish-green leaves which are larger and more incised than those of ordinary rhubarb.

There are a number of species and varieties of *Symphytum*, or comfrey, in different heights and flower colours. Comfrey is a medicinal plant, and has many uses; for example the leaves can be dried and made into a tea which is said to relieve bronchitis and coughs. A compress made by dipping a cloth into the tea is believed to aid recovery from sprained ankles and similar injuries. *Symphytum officinalis* is a useful garden plant, and is also common in some parts of the countryside. There are pinkish-white and violet species, and cultivars in beautiful sky blues. *Symphytum uplandicum*, for example, grows to a height of 60–80cm (24–32in) and has sky-blue flowers which change colour to purple. *Symphytum peregrinum* is a similar plant with similarly-coloured flowers, while *Symphytum grandiflorum* is smaller at 30cm (12in) and has white flowers. It makes ideal ground cover underneath trees, though the leaves look rather sorry for themselves after the plant has flowered in mid- to late spring, and it therefore needs to be planted among

other foliage plants. Finally, *Symphytum rubrum* is another ground-cover plant, this time with red flowers in mid- to late spring.

Lythrum varieties

Lythrum salicaria is often found alongside streams in the wild, and there are many other varieties of it. I often use *Lythrum salicaria* 'Morden's Pink'; this has bright pink flowers which are rather more ornamental than those of the species, which is very vigorous. *Lythrum salicaria* 'Brightness' is deep pink, 'The Beacon' is a deep pinkish-violet, and 'Robert' is deep crimson. There are also several varieties of *Lythrum virgatum*, which are smaller at only 60–70cm (24–28in) in height. *Lythrum virgatum* is similar in colour to *Lythrum salicaria*, but is more attractive; *Lythrum virgatum* 'Rosa Queen' is pink, and 'The Rocket' is a dark rose-red.

Right: *Hosta fortunei* 'Aureomarginata' has green leaves with yellow leaves. A single plant can cover this much ground!

The round, lobed leaves of _Bergenia_ are growing in front of a beautiful hardwood bench. The round leaf form is repeated in the _Catalpa bignoides_ 'Bungei' in the background on the right.

Right: This garden in a leafy suburb of Amsterdam had a large collection of conifers which had become too big for the garden. I reluctantly had some of them chopped down to stop them from forming a barrier between the front and back gardens. There was a busy road at the front of the house, and a canal to the left of the garden which was usually lined with people fishing. As a result, there always seemed to be someone passing by and looking into the garden, so I created a large, secluded pond where the owners could sunbathe and picnic in privacy. I then planted this area with moisture-loving plants such as brunnera, ferns, and polygonums.
The back of the pond was already planted with holly, rhododendrons, and taller trees such as beeches and conifers. The pond is now the central feature of the garden, and the garden is a beautiful collection of plants with something in flower at every time of the year.

Astilbes

Although you will see astilbes growing in a wide variety of garden situations, they are moisture-loving by nature and prefer a position beside a pond or stream in partial shade. They have unmistakable tapering, feathery panicles of flowers, which create a soft ferny effect and look particularly good beside water. They also make good plants for the far end of a small garden, where delicate, wispy plants such as these increase the apparent length of the garden.

When astilbes flower in summer, the great range of heights and flower colours becomes apparent. There is _Astilbe chinensis_ 'Amethyst', 1m (3ft) high with crimson to lilac flowers, and 'Betsy Cuperus', which is light pink and of a similar height. 'Diamant' is slightly shorter at 80cm (32in), with white flowers, and 'Erika' is about the same height, with large pink plumes. _Astilbe chinensis_ 'Pumila' is a vivid raspberry red.

There are also plenty of less tall astilbes _Astilbe_ 'Bonn' is crimson and reaches a height of about 50cm (20in); 'Deutschland' is white and 'Europa' has a large pink plume. 'Etna' is dark red, and 'Fanal' is crimson. 'Feuer' is coral red, and 'Dedersee' salmon pink. As you can see, the choice is enormous.

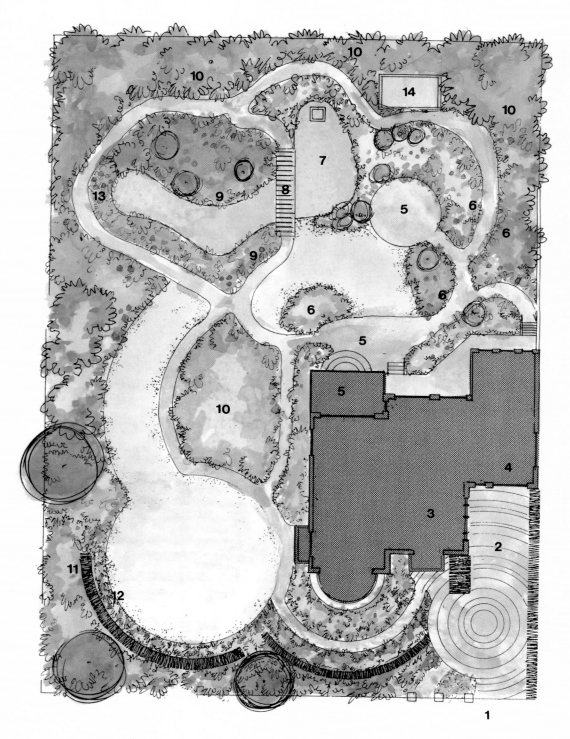

1 public road
2 front path
3 front door
4 garage
5 patios
6 borders of roses and herbaceous perennials
7 pond

8 simple wooden bridge
9 low-growing hosta
10 evergreen shrubs and a few conifers
11 curved yew hedge
12 blue hosta
13 *Petasites hybridus*
14 compost heap

CHAPTER 11

Bridges

A place to stand and contemplate nature

In some renowned gardens, the bridge is one of the central features of the whole design. A bridge is clearly more than just a way of getting from A to B; it can also arouse admiration, nostalgia, and a sense of historical continuity. A good example of a bridge which combines all of these is the one at Stourhead in Wiltshire, England.

The Roman bridge at Stourhead

A number of Roman bridges have stood the test of time in Britain, bearing testimony to the building skills of this ancient people. The Romans needed direct routes linking their main garrisons so that they could quickly assemble large numbers of troops in the event of an uprising. Where these roads crossed rivers and valleys, they built arched stone bridges. They cut the stones so that they held one another in place, and the resulting bridges were fine examples of both stonecutting and engineering.

The aim of the garden at Stourhead was to create a Roman atmosphere, and to symbolize man's life on earth. There is a spring, where life begins; a temple of love, and a mausoleum, where the embalmed body awaited the hereafter.

One of the features of Claude Monet's garden in Giverny is a green semicircular bridge covered in flowers. This bridge is inspired by the one at Giverny.

I designed this large pond at the Garden Gallery in the Dutch town of Eext. The bridge lies almost in the water, surrounded by native bog and aquatic plants.

Stepping-stones can be used to create curiosity about what lies around the next corner.

The fact that life is the passage from birth to death is represented at Stourhead by the Roman bridge. This was built using traditional methods, with stone piles and arches. One bank is planted with gunneras, and at the other end of the bridge is a row of tall, narrow conifers. These are surrounded by lawns, and there are also many trees with colourful bark and foliage, such as copper beeches.

In the distance are the slender columns of the mausoleum, and the temple is hidden behind tall rhododendrons. The garden is dominated by the huge lake, which Henry Hoare designed in the 1770s together with the rest of the garden.

Bridges of different materials

In countries where plenty of natural stone is available, stone bridges can be made fairly quickly. It is a strong material which can last for centuries if used properly, but stone bridges are expensive. A firm foundation, perhaps of stone slabs, must be dug in the muddy banks of the river or lake before the piers are constructed on either side.

Historically, making an arched bridge involved constructing a sturdy wooden framework and then covering it with pieces of stone, which tapered towards the bottom so that they formed an arch when placed side by side. Each piece was held in position by its neighbours, so that the bridge did not sag. Another method was to place heavy stone slabs across the piers to link them. Alternatively, stone bridges could be constructed using a brick bridge which was then covered in hard stone cladding.

Brick bridges

In regions where there are rivers and lakes, the clay can be shaped into bricks which are then dried by the sun and wind. This has been done throughout the world since time immemorial.

Bricks can also be used to make bridges, though the one drawback is that unlike stone, they need to be kept dry during the construction process.

In the case of stone bridges, the site can be enclosed by wooden piles so that it can be drained dry before creating firm foundations for the bricks. Like brick arches in a roof, brick bridges are built on to a wooden framework. If this is done properly, the bridge may last for centuries, and if your finances

can stretch to a brick bridge, the result can be uniquely satisfying.

Sometimes, you will see a stone base extending upwards from the water, with the piers and paving of the bridge being made of brick. In the past, brick was often replaced by stone, tiles or clay as a surface, because brick soon became rutted by the wheels of carts and carriages.

Many medieval and Renaissance castles in northern Europe have brick bridges with a central section consisting of a wooden drawbridge. In Britain, the widespread use of brick in gardens and garden structures owes a great deal to the Arts and Crafts movement in the second half of the nineteenth century, which encouraged the use of traditional skills and materials. The movement helped to bring

This Japanese-looking garden, complete with bamboo water pipe, bridge, and *Acer dissectum*, is actually in France.

about a revival in the use of brick for walls, doorframes, floors, ponds, and bridges.

The British architect Edwin Lutyens became famous for the many villas and gardens he created in association with the garden designer Gertrude Jekyll. One of these, a new villa with a new garden, was Gledstone Hall in Yorkshire. This has a long rectangular pond centred on the enormous house which Lutyens built for Amos Nelson in the 1920s. A bridge was built across the pond beside the house, and also provides partial support for the terrace. As a result, the water actually runs under the terrace

The wooden piles of this bridge have been extended upwards to form the uprights of the balustrade. The bridge has been used to cross a boggy area of the garden.

for part of the way and ends in its shadow. As you look back from the garden to the house, you see how effective brick bridges can be. Lutyens used them in a number of his other gardens, including the Deanery Garden in Sonning, Berkshire.

Wooden bridges

Wooden bridges are easy to build and relatively inexpensive, but wood is much less durable than stone or brick. It is rare for bridges to last for centuries unless they are rebuilt, because all wood eventually decays.

The exploration of new areas of the world such as China, Japan, Burma, Malaysia, and South America resulted in the increased use of hardwoods, which lasted for much longer than the oak or pine commonly used in northern Europe. Bridges made from hardwoods can be expected to last for generations.

The oak bridge at Walenburg Castle

In 1960, work began on restoring the thirteenth-century castle at Walenburg, in the Dutch province of Utrecht. The moats surrounding the two islands which comprise the site were re-excavated; one of

these houses the castle itself, and the other is the location for one of the most famous gardens in the Netherlands.

The owners of the castle decided to use oak for the two bridges, one of them linking the two islands and the other connecting the castle with the path which led to it. They had visited many British gardens, which provided a rich source of inspiration when it came to designing the bridge. The result has already been admired by tens of thousands of visitors.

One of the bridges has unusual wooden uprights set into the bottom of the moat and extending up beyond the parapet of the bridge like wooden columns, surmounted by bosses carved out of the oak. This is the only ornamentation on an otherwise beautifully simple bridge.

To prevent unauthorized visitors from entering the castle, the bridge from the entrance path to the island on which the building is located has a beautiful ornamental arch and a wooden gate, just tall enough to prevent people from climbing over it.

The waterside is planted with *Rosa* 'New Dawn', a vigorous climber which bears pale pink flowers over a long period in summer and autumn. This has spread over the parapet of the bridge and the arched gateway, and the result has everyone reaching for their cameras. The wooden bridge has already weathered to an attractive grey, and is likely to last another 30 years at least. It is difficult to imagine a finer combination of man-made and natural beauty.

A natural bridge in the water

Sometimes, a bridge needs to blend into its surroundings rather than being a distinctive architectural feature in its own right. One garden which I designed for a centuries-old farmhouse had an informal pond, for which I built a very low bridge which actually rested in the water. The bridge was made of round impregnated hardwood poles, and was partly covered in bog plants such as *Petasites hybridus*. Further along the edge of the pond, I planted bog myrtle or sweet gale, *Myrica gale*; purple loosestrife, *Lythrum salicaria*; periwinkle, *Vinca minor*, and various ferns.

The owners of this farmhouse garden were fanatical collectors of native plants and wildlife, and there is

What looks like a flimsy old bridge in fact has a sturdy iron framework.

which are hidden from view using large rocks, and it was this idea which I subsequently used for the garden in Denmark.

The photographer of this book, Philippe Perdereau, discovered a beautiful wooden bridge behind the house of the British garden designer Anthony Paul. This has a large, informal pond crossed by a series of simple bridges made of planks, a common feature in old Japanese gardens.

Each consists of two or three thick planks of similar size placed side by side, and the bridges are then arranged in staggered positions across the pond; it is important that they are placed along either side of a more or less straight line.

The construction of the bridges is simple and ingenious. Two stakes are driven into the ground at each end of the bridge, and these are then linked by a cross-piece, on top of which the planks themselves are placed. The uprights have been left protruding slightly above the planks, creating variety and emphasizing the hand-made nature of the bridge. I have seen this idea being used in two old gardens in Japan; one in Tokyo, and the other in Okayama.

always something new to be discovered in this natural-looking pond, which in fact was made using a PVC liner. This was covered in a deep layer of earth, so that the plants could root in the bottom of the pond.

A Japanese-style bridge in England

I have designed many Japanese gardens, the most recent of which was for the Danish company Bruhn in Herlev, a suburb of Copenhagen. I installed a carved black granite bridge across the large pond, and used the same material for the steps up to the tea-house, which I also designed.

The result was an authentic-looking garden, with a combination of white gravel, solitary stones, and neatly pruned pine trees. My source of inspiration was Shugakuin, the emperor's garden in Kyoto, where two simple houses were built for the emperor and his wife, nestling amid the trees on a fairly steep hillside. The garden also includes private apartments

The outlines of this bridge have been softened by yellow flags (right) and *Peltiphyllum peltatum* (left).

A tumbledown pile of stone slabs makes a simple, romantic bridge across a pond covered in water lilies

The bridges in Korakuen Park, Tokyo

There are two main currents in Japanese garden design, both derived from the same origins. The idea behind all Japanese gardens is always to use nature as an example and reproduce it in more or less stylized form. Unlike western gardens, there is no desire to shape nature into architectural forms such as hedges and topiary. Ponds, paths, and groups of plants are designed in flowing curves rather than straight lines.

In the Zen style of gardening, the forms are so simplified that the natural origins of the garden are often not immediately apparent, but they are there all the same. The garden is simplified as much as possible, to create a place for meditation with no complex or intricate forms to distract the visitor.

Tokyo's Korakuen Park has many small hills, and lakes designed for walking around. The park is divided into sections, each with its own separate style and each intended to represent one of the most beautiful areas of Japan. One section is based on the use of bridges, which form part of a paddy field placed there as a reminder of Japan's rural traditions. The bridges cross a pond, planted with *Iris*

kaempferi so that the plants can be enjoyed from close up.

Staggered bridges in Okayama

Most bridges are designed to lead directly from one side of a pond or river to the other, but when I visited the Korakuen garden in Okayama I found that this need not necessarily be the case. Here, the purpose of the bridge has been to provide not the quickest, but the most interesting route across a stream, again planted with Japanese irises. The planks have been laid in a more or less zigzag arrangement, with the first at right angles to the bank, and the second laid diagonally on top of it. The third is placed diagonally on top of the second, and so on, creating a zigzag pattern. The idea is that each board forces the visitor to look at the water and the plants from a different angle. This works very well, but it took a long time to cross the water; I found myself constantly stopping to take photographs of this beautiful scene.

This small, formal bridge which I designed for a garden in the Netherlands is given added interest by the plants trained over it.

The famous bridge at Giverny

Here, old and new have been combined, with an unusual bridge of planks and a display of contemporary sculpture.

The French impressionist painter Claude Monet first saw his dream house from a train. He got off at the next station and rented this long, stuccoed building as a summer home in which to paint.

Eventually, he bought the house, and it became his permanent home. Monet had two great loves in life apart from painting: one was cooking, as his recipe book shows, and the other was colourful flowers. He painted many pictures of his flower garden, full of reds, pinks, yellows, and oranges. Once the flower garden behind the house was complete, he bought a plot of land beside a river across the road. He dug a large pond and then diverted the river on to his land, giving him an area of fresh, flowing water on which

Walenburg Castle is one of the finest gardens in the Netherlands. It is owned by the Dutch Gardens Foundation and is open to the public on a few days a year.

The garden of Walenburg Castle from the tower, showing the different compartments of the garden arranged in the shape of a cross.

he planted large groups of differently coloured water lilies. Monet painted these in a series of huge canvases, the "Water lilies", which became world-famous.

Monet went on to build a bridge across part of the pond, which was painted green and was recorded for posterity along with the water lilies in his paintings. It is a graceful semi-circular structure which is reflected in the water below when viewed from the side, thus creating a circle. The bridge has a wooden parapet, with an iron palisade above it following the semicircle of the bridge. Both the parapet and the palisade are covered in the fragrant flowers of *Wisteria sinensis* and its white cultivar, 'Alba'.

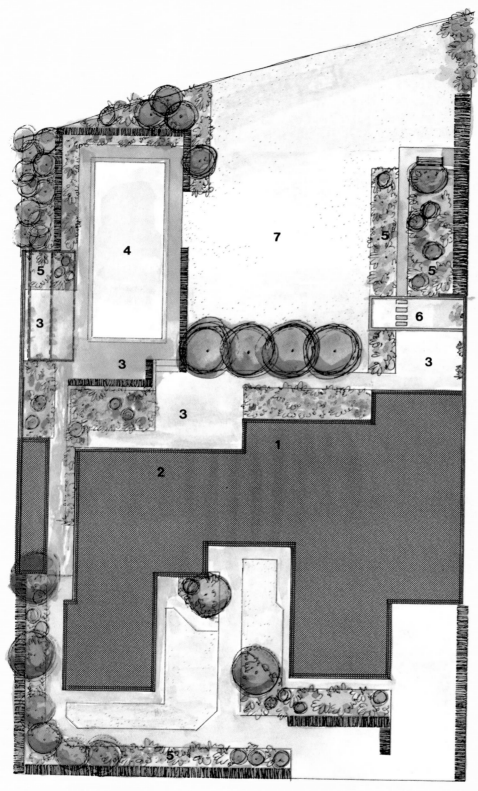

Left: This garden has both a swimming-pool and a pond (6) with stepping stones over it. The back door leads out on to a patio (3), which serves as an extra room to the house. Water flows into the pond from stone channels set into the wall, and stepping-stones lead across the pond and on to a grass path with flower borders on either side. On the left of the garden is the sunken swimming-pool, surrounded on three sides by hedges of various heights. There is also a sunken patio with a pergola covered in white and apricot-coloured flowers, harmonizing beautifully with the grass and emerald green water.

1 house
2 bedroom
3 patios on various levels
4 swimming-pool
5 herbaceous perennials
6 long, narrow pond with stepping-stones
7 lawn

Acknowledgements

The photographer and publisher would like to thank all the garden owners and designers who allowed their gardens to be photographed.

Special thanks are due to the following:

FRANCE
Villa Noailles, Grasse (p. 14)
M. and Mme. Colette Sainte-Beuve, Planbessin, Calvados (pp. 60, 62, 63, 67, 82, 92, 122, 129)
M. and Mme. Chevalier Frinault, Orléans (pp. 88, 89)
M. and Mme. Peche, Brittany (p. 90)
Erwan Tymen (designer), Brittany (p. 92)
M. and Mme. Baizet, Saône et Loire (p. 93)
M. Sermadiras, Eyrignac, Dordogne (pp. 103, 104)
M. and Mme. Plottier, Valbonne (p. 113)
M. and Mme. Cotelle, Normandy (p. 122)

BELGIUM
M. and Mme. d'Assembourg; designed by Jacques Wirtz (pp. 10, 26, 40, 97, 105)
Mme. Jacquemin, Les Sept Collines (pp. 37, 47, 106)
André van Vassenhove (designer), Bruges (p. 68)

GREAT BRITAIN
Hascombe Court, Surrey (p. 9)
Bodnant Garden, Gwynedd (pp. 18, 74)
Ladham House, Kent (pp. 18, 44)
Cobblers, Sussex (pp. 23, 24, 94)
Northbourne Court, Kent (pp. 25, 61)
Coke's Barn, West Sussex (p. 27)
Hazelbury Manor Gardens, Wiltshire (pp. 30, 38)
Garsington Manor, Oxfordshire (p. 32)
Mottisfont Abbey Garden, Hampshire (pp. 34, 35, 98)
The Old Rectory, Berkshire (p. 43)
Beth Chatto Gardens, Essex (pp. 45, 46, 54, 72, 81, 126, 127, 131)
Brook Cottage, Oxfordshire (pp. 58, 85)
Hodnet Hall Gardens, Shropshire (pp. 48, 49, 79, 86, 114, 130)

Lower Hall, Shropshire (pp. 53, 58, 59, 104, 123, 134, 135)
Furzey Gardens, Hampshire (pp. 70, 71)
Weeks Farm, Kent (pp. 84, 140)
Mill House, West Sussex (pp. 91, 139)
Chenies Manor House, Buckinghamshire (p. 100)
Church Hill Gardens, Oxfordshire (p. 138)
The Hannah Peschar Gallery Garden, Surrey (pp. 41, 80, 81, 96, 120, 121, 124, 139, 141)
The Royal Horticultural Society's Garden, Wisley, Surrey (p. 29)

NETHERLANDS
Dhr. Jaap Nieuwenhuis, Overijssel (p. 11)
Dhr. Joop Braam, Noord-Brabant (p. 64)
Dhr. and Mw. De Gruyter; designed by A.J. van der Horst (p. 60)
Dhr. and Mw. Dekker, Zeeland (p. 65)
Dhr. and Mw. Branden, Zeeland (pp. 19, 20, 21, 22, 39, 132)
Dhr. and Mw. Geluk, Zeeland (p. 26)
Dhr. and Mw. Meyburg, Noord-Brabant (pp. 30, 41, 43)
Dhr. and Mw. Meyer, Zeeland (pp. 31, 73, 95, 96, 99, 101, 115, 128, 140)
Pieter Baak and Frank Linschoten, Drenthe (p. 136)
Walenburg, Utrecht (pp. 142, 108, 109)